To Mimi

A Plain Man's Guide
to
The Glorious Revolution
1688

Mary Howarth

23 July 1988

Front Cover Illustration
William, Prince of Orange, after landing at Torbay on 5th November, 1688. This contemporary portrait by the Dutchman J. Wyck is in the National Maritime Museum at Greenwich. In the original painting some of the 4,000 horses landed may be seen swimming ashore, steered by men in boats with a guide-line. A similar, more familiar portrait, by the same artist shows William at the battle of the Boyne, on a black horse facing to the right.
Back Cover Illustration
James Francis Edward Stuart, aged twelve months. (Scottish National Portrait Gallery.)

● Key towns where the Revolution was declared, November 1688.

In brackets the leaders who declared for William there: Chester and Manchester (Delamere); Derby and Nottingham (Devonshire); York (Danby); Newcastle-upon-Tyne (Lumley); Oxford and Mid Thames Valley (Lovelace); Bristol (Shrewsbury and Bishop Trelawney); Norwich (Duke of Norfolk); Hull (Officers of the garrison and Magistrates of the Town); Worcester (Herbert of Charbury and Harley).

A Plain Man's Guide
to
The Glorious Revolution
1688

by

MARY HOWARTH

Regency Press (London & New York) Ltd.
125 High Holborn, London WC1V 6QA

To
James Howarth
my late husband
whose library of books
has been invaluable to me
in my studies for this work

ISBN 0 7212 0704 9

Printed and bound in Great Britain by
Buckland Press Ltd., Dover, Kent.

Contents

List of Illustrations

Front Cover: William at Torbay by J. Wyck (National Maritime Museum)
Back Cover: James Francis Edward Stuart, aged twelve months (Scottish National Portrait Gallery)

Maps:

A Note on Dates

Until 1752, when we adopted the Gregorian calendar, Britain still used the Julian or Old Style calendar introduced by Julius Caesar in 45 B.C. It was ten days behind the Gregorian or New Style calendar introduced by Pope Gregory and used on the Continent since 1582. To simplify I have used only Old Style for all dates.

CHATSWORTH

Preface
by His Grace The Duke of Devonshire

It gives me great pleasure to write a preface to Mrs. Howarth's book on the Glorious Revolution, the tercentenary of which is 1988.

My family did extremely well out of the Revolution and we are much indebted to William and Mary. William Cavendish, the 4th Earl of Devonshire, later to become the 1st Duke of Devonshire, was a prominent figure at Court, but fell out with King James II over the latter's leaning towards the Roman Catholic faith. In the end he was banished from Court circles and retired to Chatsworth. He spent his enforced leisure in rebuilding Chatsworth, gradually converting Bess of Hardwick's Elizabethan house into the splendid classical building which stands to this day.

He employed the architect, Talman, to help him in this work, and at the same time he was active in plotting the downfall of the King, with his chief associates, Danby and d'Arcy. When the time arrived, he called upon the citizens of the area to come out in support of William and Mary. The house where he signed the proclamation still stands in Whittington, North Derbyshire, and to this day it is known as Revolution House.

William and Mary showed their gratitude by creating William Cavendish 1st Duke of Devonshire, and lavished many gifts on him, including a handsome silver chandelier, an ornate silver gilt dressing table set and a magnificent set of Dutch Delft china.

But for William and Mary, I would not be writing this in my sitting room at Chatsworth, with its incomparable view. I have every intention of taking an active part in the Tercentenary celebrations, I have much to celebrate.

Devonshire

Acknowledgements

The author would like to thank Mr. Francis Bennion for kindly reading the typescript of this book, and for his valuable help in making criticisms and corrections. Any errors of fact are however entirely her own.

She would also like to thank the staffs of the local public libraries at Henley-on-Thames and Maidenhead for their unfailing courtesy and assistance, and likewise Frances Dunkel and Duncan Smith of the Prints and Drawings Room at the British Museum for help beyond the call of duty in her researching the pictures for illustrations. Also to be thanked are Lindsey Macfarlane at the National Maritime Museum, the Registrar of the Queen's Pictures at St. James's Palace, the custodians of the Glasgow Art Gallery, the National Portrait Gallery of Scotland, and local county and city archivists.

Mary Howarth

Hurley, Berkshire
April 1988

CHAPTER ONE

Road to Revolution

The 1688 Glorious Revolution in Britain broke the hereditary succession to the Crown and re-established the Monarchy and the Constitution on a new statutory basis, with the King-in-Parliament instead of the King alone as sovereign, and the King's power to make or suspend laws, by virtue of a mystical divine right, extinguished.

It significantly altered the status of the Monarch from that of an absolute Sovereign ruling by his own personal directive as the hereditary chief executive of his government, to that virtually of an hereditary president set above, but subject to, his Parliament.

His place in the law-making process was however secured, and linked to the ancient Anglo-Saxon constitution, because the laws made by the King-in-Parliament are made in the name of the Sovereign too and are not valid until they have received the Royal Assent.

Since 1688 therefore, the British Constitution may be compared to a three-piered interdependent structure like the Forth Bridge, of King, Parliament and People, no one part of which can function legally without the participation and consent of the others. Therein lies its strength and permanence.

How and why did the Glorious Revolution happen? Who started and led it? How long did it last and how exactly was it settled? Why indeed was it Glorious?

To understand the reasons for this dramatic upheaval in our constitutional history, we must know someting of the sequence of events which preceded and produced it. It was really the culmination of the long struggle between the Stuart kings and the more radical members of Parliament, especially of the House of Commons, which lasted most of the seventeenth century.

The cause of this struggle was basically a clash between two conflicting and incompatible ideas about the nature and function of monarchy. The Stuart kings believed as an article of faith that an hereditary king was born with a divine right to rule, a right sanctified by the Church in the sacrament of anointing the sovereign at his coronation, by which solemn rite he is set apart from and above his subjects.

Thus the king's will, as an instrument or agent of God's will, was law and paramount, and actively to contest it on important issues, especially touching religion, was by definition sedition or rebellion. And religion, whether Britain should be a Protestant or Catholic country, became under James II the burning issue which both provoked and was settled by the Glorious Revolution.

The Stuart motto epitomised their deeply-held belief in divine right—*Non desideriis hominum sed voluntate Dei*—not by the desires of men but by the Will of God.

The Parliamentarians or radicals of the seventeenth century believed no less fervently that government was a secular not a religious institution, an unwritten social contract, in effect a bargain, between King and people. In return for their allegiance the King must govern in accordance with the wishes of his subjects through their elected representatives in Parliament—that is, in accordance with the laws made by Parliament.

This was then a new and revolutionary concept. The Stuart kings would not or could not grasp such a notion, and were consequently often at loggerheads with their Parliaments. Charles I was adamant in his belief that "a sovereign and a subject are quite different things." For a subject even to claim the right to petition the king, as the bolder spirits did, was regarded by him as inadmissible.

Many loyal subjects however, both in and out of Parliament, upheld the King's belief that his royal prerogative was inviolable and that it was wrong to contest the way in which the King chose to rule. This was called the doctrine of non-resistance.

The road to revolution is therefore marked, as with milestones, by laws passed by Parliament enacting the claims of the Commons of England to their rights and liberties, in opposition to the Stuart kings' sometimes contemptuous disregard or denial of those self-same rights and liberties.

These milestones may be listed as follows:

1.

Petition to James I 1621, presenting a resolution passed by the House of Commons, protesting against the King's violation of their privileges and "undoubted" rights to freedom of speech and debate concerning the conduct and policies of the King's government (vis-à-vis Spain). The King's answer to this was to tear the Petition out of the Commons journal with his own hand.

2.

Petition of Right 1628 to Charles I, passed as a law by Parliament, re-affirming the 1621 claims to freedom of speech and debate, and declaring arbitrary imprisonment without trial and taxation without consent of Parliament, to be unlawful. Charles reluctantly gave his Royal Assent to this Act, but only because he needed money (legitimately enough for the defence of the realm), insisting that he was accountable only to God, not to Parliament, and that his assent did not imply any surrender of his royal prerogative.

3.

The Grand Remonstrance 1641 passed by the Commons with a majority however of only eleven. It was a massive and comprehensive attack on the monarchy listing 206 grievances against the King's government in violation of their rights and liberties, and stipulating the then revolutionary idea that Parliament should choose the King's advisers. This was considered by many as a preposterous denial of the King's "ancient rights" and "natural liberties", hence the narrow majority.

4.

The Civil War 1642-51 between King and Parliament over this general issue, whether the King or Parliament was paramount in the realm.

5.

Execution of Charles I on 30th January, 1649 for "High Treason and other high Crymes" against his people, as represented by Parliament. His death warrant was signed by 59 Parliamentarians, including O. Cromwell. The King conducted himself with great courage and dignity throughout his trial and execution. He considered himself, as did many of his loyal subjects, a martyr to his belief in his divine right to royal paramountcy.

CHAPTER TWO

The Republican Experiment

The Civil War was followed by the unprecedented experiment in republicanism called the Commonwealth, under the rebel leader Oliver Cromwell. It was a one-off in this country—in 1,300-plus years of monarchical government it had never been tried before and has never been tried since.

In February 1649, after the execution of the King and the abolition of his office—including the hasty annulment, on the morning of his father's execution, of Charles II's hereditary succession—the House of Commons also abolished the House of Lords as "useless and dangerous". They then appointed a Council of State headed by Cromwell, a military junta, on their own say-so without legal authority, with sub-committees acting as departments of state under it.

Thus the new republican system of government consisted of Parliament, now a single-chamber body, and its executive branch the Council of State chaired by Cromwell. On 19th May it passed its first Act, declaring and constituting the People of England to be a Commonwealth and a free State, a high-sounding but impersonal concept without precedent and with no basis in law.

There was of course no popular consent for this revolutionary change in the Constitution; consent was not even sought, far less obtained by a general election. Royalists for instance had not consented to the murder of the King, or to the subsequent usurpation of his powers by the Commons and Council of State.

The oath of allegiance to the King was replaced by a new oath of allegiance to the Commonwealth, specific and unequivocal, thus:

> "I do declare and promise that I will be true and faithful to the Commonwealth of England as now established, without a King or House of Lords."

In public places and churches the Royal Arms were replaced by the new arms of the Commonwealth, the actual changeover being overseen locally by Justices of the Peace and churchwardens. A new Great Seal and coinage were likewise struck, bearing impersonal symbols of the Commonwealth instead of the head of the King.

In effect the Act of 19th May, 1649:

"constituted the House of Commons [nicknamed the Rump Parliament because it was composed of the surviving members of the Long Parliament originally called by Charles I nine years before] as the supreme [and sole] source of power in the realm without even a King or House of Lords to check it."*

Nor was any limit set to the duration of this Rump Parliament; in theory it could prolong itself indefinitely if it so wished. After sitting for four years it did try to do precisely that, but was thwarted by Cromwell himself in a famous and dramatic intervention. For in April 1653 the Rump decided, despite a pledge to the contrary, to prolong itself indefinitely.

Cromwell, infuriated at this breaking of its promise to dissolve itself by a Bill already under discussion and expectedly shortly to become an Act, rushed, purple with rage, from Whitehall to St. Stephen's Chapel—then the House of Commons—ordered the soldiers of the guard to remove the Mace—"this Bauble"—from the Table, snatched the Bill of Dissolution lying there and stormed off with it, thus forcibly himself dissolving the Rump Parliament.

The document disappeared for ever, and with it the journal of the House for that day, so what it actually contained is unknown.

Three months later, on 4th July, 1653, a new House of Commons was installed, dubbed by the wags "Barebone's Parliament" after the quaintly named Mr. Praise-God Barbon, junior member for the City of London. This House of one hundred and fifty members, or more accurately Assembly of Nominees, was not elected by the People of England in whose name it sat, but nominated by Cromwell and his Council of State.

The method of nomination was pure rule of thumb, owing nothing to law or precedent. Independent ministers (of religion) in England and Wales, in consultation with their congregations, submitted names from which Cromwell and his Council chose the members to sit in the nominated Assembly. Although obviously mostly Non-Conformists, they were nevertheless fairly representative of various interests.

Cromwell addressed the first meeting of this "Barebone's Representative"—the name Parliament was at first coyly avoided—probably in the Council Chamber of Whitehall Palace. Later it moved to St. Stephen's Chapel, thus boldly but improperly

*Cromwell: Our Chief of Men by Antonia Fraser.

equating itself with a properly elected House of Commons.

In his speech Cromwell announced a new republican constitution called the *Instrument of Government,* which in effect devolved some of his own self-assumed powers as virtual dictator on the Assembly, but invested him with supreme power as its chief executive, with a Council of State of twenty-one members to serve for life. Any vacancies which inevitably occurred were to be filled by him from a list of six nominees chosen by the House.

The legislative power was vested in the Assembly, but the chief executive—that is, Cromwell himself—was empowered to suspend the passing of any Act for twenty days if he thought fit.* Parliaments were to be held at least once in every three years, and not to be dissolved until they had sat for a minimum of five lunar months.

Later a chicken-and-egg argument arose between Cromwell and the nominated Assembly. He maintained that it drew its powers from him, "the authority who called you", but the Parliament held that he drew his powers as chief executive from it. It was virtually the old bone of contention surfacing again, whether the chief executive (formerly the King) or the Parliament as legislature was paramount in the realm.

Various artificial titles as substitute for King were mooted for Cromwell as chief executive—Governor, Imperator, Generalissimo— but eventually the more benign-sounding Lord Protector was chosen, cosily evocative of a father-figure like the uncle-proxies, also called Lord Protector, who ruled during the minority of the boy-Kings Henry VI and Edward VI.

The following year, on 3rd September, 1654, the first elected Protectorate Parliament met, of four hundred members from England and Wales, plus thirty "fraternal delegates" from Scotland and thirty from Ireland. Although fifty years in advance of the Union of Scottish and English Parliaments, this was a laudable dry-run for the unitary United Kingdom Parliament which was eventually, and successfully, established in 1707.

Oliver was conveyed in right royal style from Whitehall to St. Stephen's in a "very gorgeous coach" purpose-built for him, to open the new single-chamber Parliament from a "throne" also specially made for him. He was like a King in all but name and pedigree.

---

*In 1787 the American constitution-makers copied this in the Presidential veto.

This first Protectorate Parliament was dissolved by Cromwell after the five statutory lunar months. The second and last did not meet until eighteen months later.

On 29th March, 1657, two and a half years later and eight years after the murder of King Charles, in the very Banqueting House from where the martyr King had stepped out so bravely to the block, Cromwell, the chief regicide, was actually offered, by the Speaker of the House of Commons, the title of King; packaged with a second constitutional instrument clumsily entitled the *Humble Petition and Advice,* which superseded the *Instrument of Government* as the purported legal basis for the republican government.

This second statute restored the House of Lords and, in effect, the old two-chamber constitution in an amended form, with the Protector in lieu of the King in all but title and indeed very nearly in title as well.

For five weeks Cromwell hesitated in an agony of indecision whether or not to accept the Speaker's offer of the royal title. A crown re-made from some of the jewels from Charles I's ancient Crown of England, destroyed in 1649, was probably actually made for him. A contemporary print shows him wearing a crown and ermine.

The Speaker's committee, impatient for a decision, at last got him to the table only to be told that he would not accept the title of King. The army and some of his family were against it; and moreover the headless ghost of Charles I must surely have haunted and taunted him in the midnight hour and influenced his decision to reject it.

So, on 26th June, 1657, the second republican constitution was inaugurated in Westminster Hall with Cromwell still as Lord Protector not King, in a ceremony however akin to a coronation in every respect except for the absence of Crown, Orb and anointing. Sword of State and Sceptre were both presented to him, an oath taken by him, and he even sat in the "chair of Scotland" as generations of hereditary Scottish kings had sat before him.

The "chair of Scotland" was not the English Coronation chair specially made for Edward I to hold the fabled Stone of Destiny which he (Edward) had removed from Scone to London in 1296, but the "Chair of State" of the pre-Union kings of Scotland, of equal antiquity, which General Monk had plundered after the battle of Dunbar in 1650. But for the audacity and ingenuity of a resourceful Scottish lady, Monk would have removed to England the Crown and Regalia of Scotland as well. (See story on page 105.)

The Scots did not at first accept Cromwell or the Commonwealth republic, and on 1st January, 1651, three months after the rout of the Scottish opposition army at the battle of Dunbar, Charles II was crowned at Scone as King of Scotland—the last time that ancient and lovely Crown was used.

Despite Cromwell's popular image as a ruthless Roundhead dictator, he was an able ruler of both England and Scotland who restored England's standing abroad and launched her as a world trading and seafaring power. As Andrew Marvell put it,

"Though his government did a tyrant resemble
He made England great and his enemies tremble."

The *Humble Petition and Advice* had decreed that "King" Oliver should name his elder surviving son Richard as his successor, thus establishing a new "royal" dynasty. But he never did, probably because he was acutely aware of the inadequacies of poor dear "Troublesome Dick".

After Oliver's death however, on 3rd September, 1658, the Council of State invited Richard Cromwell to be the new Lord Protector, on the slender justification, probably invented, that they had detected a vague nod from Old Noll in his dying moment that this was indeed his nominee for the job.

He was buried like the king he would secretly like to have been in life—Crown, Orb and Sceptre were displayed on his ermine-robed effigy at his lying-in-state in Somerset House, and later placed with the effigy in Westminster Abbey, where he was buried.

At the Restoration his body was dug up, then hung and quartered at Tyburn. His head was stuck on a pole outside Westminster Hall where it remained for twenty-five years until it was blown down in a gale. It is now buried in a secret place at Sidney Sussex College at Cambridge.

Poor Richard Cromwell lasted only eight months in his father's shoes. The following year, in May 1659, after moves for a Restoration of King Charles II had been instigated by General Monk, a Convention Parliament—that is, one not summoned by the Sovereign— was nominated by the Rump or surviving members of the Long Parliament. The Convention Parliament then invited Charles II to return to his inheritance.

To be exact, the Long Parliament first met on 3rd November, 1640 and dissolved itself nearly twenty years later on 16th March, 1660, after appointing the Convention Parliament to meet on 25th April following.

The summoning or dissolving of all parliaments during the Commonwealth by Oliver or Richard Cromwell was discounted as null and void after the Restoration, because it was not done by the Sovereign.

The fumbling experiment of the Commonwealth republic failed, but at least it eliminated republicanism as an acceptable alternative to monarchy in the search for a workable solution to the constitutional problems of the seventeenth century; caused by the emergence of an ever stronger House of Commons challenging King and House of Lords for a bigger share in the government of the country.

The Cromwellians who tried the experiment were really searching for the magic sesame, the key to the formula which was so brilliantly devised in 1689 after the glorious and bloodless revolution.

It was glorious not only because, as we shall see, it re-established beyond argument and without bloodshed the Protestant ascendancy in Britain; but because it reconciled and incorporated, in a matter of weeks, an hereditary monarchy with parliamentary sovereignty, which twenty years of civil war and republican government had signally failed satisfactorily to accomplish.

CHAPTER THREE

The Monarchy Restored

So, amid scenes of unparalleled relief and rejoicing, Charles II returned from his eleven-year exile in Holland. He landed at Dover on 25th May, 1660 and proceeded in a triumphant progress via Canterbury and Rochester to enter London on 29th May, his thirtieth birthday.

The hated and unnatural republican strait-jacket was cast off, the people let their hair down and cheered and danced for joy. The fountains ran with wine, the King had "come into his own again", the bejewelled Crown and royal regalia re-appeared, colourful pageantry returned to the streets of London and gorgeous gold plate to the Palace table.

The original Crown of St. Edward the Confessor (reigned 1042-1066) had been destroyed by order of Cromwell's parliamentary commissioners in 1649. Some of the gold and jewels survived however—it is thought they were used in the crown made for Cromwell—and were re-fashioned into a new St. Edward's Crown made for Charles II and still used at coronations, the last time at that of the Queen in 1953.

The decade of republicanism faded like a bad nightmare almost as though it had never been. It was dull, joyless, soulless and even, in retrospect, illegal. After the Restoration all the Acts passed by the republican parliaments were declared null and void because they had not received the Royal Assent.

Charles was granted by Parliament a revenue of £1,200,000 to run the country, less than that allowed for Cromwell.

Unlike his father and the younger brother who succeeded him, he was a shrewd and clever politician, an able chief executive of his own government. Instead of contesting his Parliaments head-on as they so often did, he handled and controlled them by more subtle, some might say devious and unscrupulous, means.

This applied also to his dealings with the Continental Powers, which swung from enmity against to alliance with France, partly through the agency of his enchanting young sister, fourteen years his junior—the French-reared Henriette-Anne (Minette), Duchess of Orleans, who was married to the brother of Louis XIV.

Continental alignments at that time changed bewilderingly like a game of musical chairs, as Catholic France jostled for ascendancy in Europe, and the other Powers sought to contain her. In 1666 Louis XIV, in an unnatural alliance with Protestant Holland, declared war against England and in June 1667 the Dutch navy actually penetrated into the Medway, burning the royal ships at anchor there. Peace was patched together a month later.

In 1668 the Franco-Dutch alliance was reversed when England, Holland and Sweden, the main Protestant Powers, lined up against Catholic France to check Louis's pretensions, in the Triple Alliance. Within months however Charles II blithely accepted a bribe of £18,000 from Louis to renege on the treaty and join with France against Holland, thus betraying his nephew William of Orange, now eighteen and shaping up for the leadership of his country.

Two years later, when the Treaty of Dover was signed to seal the deal between England and France—Henriette-Anne met her brother at Dover to secure it—Charles and Louis agreed on a secret clause, known only to the Catholic Lords Clifford and Arlington in England, that

Louis would pay his cousin £200,000 a year if Charles openly declared himself a Catholic, "as soon as the welfare of his kingdom will permit"—an escape clause, probably inserted by him, which he made full use of. This was in fact part of a separate and secret treaty signed on 22nd May, 1670, seven months before the public treaty was signed the following December.

To become a Catholic Charles would have had to break his coronation oath to uphold the Anglican church. In the event he never did so, probably deceiving Louis and even his sister by pretending that he ever would; and only on his death-bed, when it no longer had political significance, did he become a Catholic.

The public Treaty of Dover detailed the unscrupulous Anglo-French plans for a joint attack on the United Provinces; France by land through the Spanish Netherlands (now Belgium) and England by sea with fifty ships and six thousand soldiers, plus another thirty French ships and £300,000 from Louis.

The coastal province of Zeeland and three islands at the mouth of the Scheldt were to go to England at the intended carve-up of the Dutch republic between England and France.

On 6th April, 1672 Charles deliberately provoked the war by ordering the royal navy to attack a Dutch merchant fleet homeward-bound from the Middle East. Next day Louis XIV, the Most Christian King, heading a French army 120,000 strong, left Paris and swept north via Charleroi to cross the Rhine near Nimegen and enter the Dutch republic by mid-June.

But William of Orange, only twenty-one and already Captain and Admiral-General of the Dutch forces, thwarted the invasion by ordering the dykes to be opened, thus flooding his frontier lands in the face of the disconcerted French. This daring stroke made his name as a leader in Europe, a Protestant boy David able to defy and defeat the Catholic Goliath of Louis XIV. On 8th July, 1672, in recognition of his prowess, William was made the civilian as well as the military head of the United Provinces.

There were three separate Anglo-Dutch wars in twenty-two years, basically over trade and colonial rivalries—in 1652-54 under Cromwell, 1666-67 and 1672-74 under Charles II. That Dutch William should be welcomed with an army in 1688 and offered the Crowns of England and Scotland is therefore all the more remarkable.

In 1675 Louis paid Charles another £75,000 annually in return for his continued support against the Dutch. A contemporary cartoon shows him running after the King with his money bags. In all, during his reign, Charles received from his French cousin a total of approximately £746,000, roughly half his annual revenue from Parliament, of which the notorious Dover treaty deal accounted for about eighty per cent.

Thus Louis's financial largesse enabled Charles to prorogue Parliament at will, allowing him more freedom to pursue his suspect and unpopular pro-Catholic French policy without having to tailor it too closely, as would otherwise have been the case, to parliamentary approval.

The main weapon used by all the Stuart kings in their dealings with Parliament was the absolute royal power to prorogue or dissolve them as and when it suited the King to do so. There was no law against it and no law requiring the King as chief executive of his government to call a Parliament. The Stuart kings, and indeed Cromwell, could and sometimes did rule without one, quite legally, advised only by their Privy Councillors chosen by themselves from members of both Houses or of neither.

The main weapon used by every Parliament against the Stuart kings was its equally effective power to control the purse strings, to withhold the grant of supply or money until grievances had been redressed or royal policies trimmed to Parliament's wishes. These weapons were constantly invoked against each other in retaliatory moves by both King and Parliament. It was the name of the game in those days.

The Stuart period seems indeed to be a story of mutual arm-twisting between King and Parliament, each wielding its own powers as muscle, as between two equally determined, but not necessarily hostile, wrestlers. A reflection of this mutual political arm-twisting between the chief executive and the legislature may be seen today between the United States President and his Congress.

The British people have a deep respect for the monarchy and the hereditary succession, and equally for the laws of the land. In 1688, with memories of the tragedy and bloodshed of the Civil War still green, they were even more reluctant to settle major issues by revolutionary means, especially if this involved another clash of wills between Parliament and the Sovereign.

That they were forced to do so again in the lifetime of many who had seen the nine-years-long Civil War and the murder of the King—which had seemingly tilted the balance between King and Parliament in the latter's favour—must mean that there was some exceptional provocation or some exceptional circumstances, or both.

What that provocation was, and what those exceptional circumstances were, we will now find out. On both counts the issue was religion—whether in effect Britain should remain a Protestant or become a Catholic country again.

CHAPTER FOUR

Protestants and Catholics in the 17th Century

It must first be explained that, in the time of Charles II and James II, Roman Catholics were hated and opposed in Britain on political as much as on religious grounds. They were regarded as a subversive minority within the realm, actively peddling through their Jesuit priests a foreign politico-religious dogma which might eventually be imposed upon their Protestant compatriots. They were consequently eyed with fear and suspicion very much as Communists are today, owing, or thought to owe, ultimate allegiance not to King and country but to a foreign overlord—the Pope.

And the Papacy then was a major political force in European affairs, in effect of Great Power status itself, exchanging envoys with the leading Roman Catholic countries like Austria, France and Spain; but not, since the Reformation, with Protestant Britain.

The dominant Roman Catholic ruler in Europe in the second half of the seventeenth century was Louis XIV of France, styled the Most Christian King, whose ambition it was to make England into a Catholic satellite of France as a stepping-stone to his ultimate aim—the overlordship of Europe.

Louis was a first cousin of Charles and James Stuart—their mother Queen Henrietta Maria being a sister of Louis XIII—and he exploited the Catholic sympathies of his royal cousins and the Catholic minority in England—a mere 100,000 or about two per cent of the then total

Louis XIV of France, first cousin of Charles II and James II. He became King at the age of eight in 1643 and reigned for 72 years. He wanted to make England into a Catholic satellite of France as a stepping-stone to the overlordship of Europe. Portrait by Jean de la Haye.

Woodcut cartoon from a contemporary political broadsheet. It depicts the Pope exhorting Englishmen to betray their country. The animals' heads represent the Catholic monarchies of Europe led by the Cockerel (France). Similar cartoons constantly depicted "popery" as synonymous with subversion and slavery.

population of five and a half million*—to procure this end.

James II was an extreme and obsessive Catholic convert. Unlike his cynical and clever brother, who carefully concealed his papist leanings, James openly flaunted his and was sometimes, unwittingly, used as a tool of his French cousin in furthering Louis XIV's ambitions.

So "popery" then, like Communism today, was equated with political enslavement and the subversion of Britain's freedom and independence by the foreign domination of Catholic France. In the House of Lords the Earl of Shaftesbury, Lord Chancellor to Charles II, voiced the then general belief, constantly depicted in political cartoons of the time, that "popery and slavery go hand in hand."

In our day this might equally be said of Communism, with Russia posing the threat to our freedom and independence which France then did; hence, after the Catholic zealot James II had acceded to the

---

*The population of Scotland was then one million, with the Catholic minority mostly north of the Forth.

Throne, the deep misgivings of the Protestant majority of his people about the security and independence of their country, and the vehement and sometimes extreme opposition to popery by patriotic subjects.

All references to popery or Catholicism in the previous and following chapters must therefore be understood in this seventeenth century political context, not as anti-papist religious prejudice in a modern sense.

CHAPTER FIVE

The Test Acts and Exclusion Bills

In 1672 James, then Duke of York and heir presumptive to his brother Charles II, openly declared himself a Roman Catholic and was publicly received into that Church. This alarmed and outraged the majority of people. It was as contentious and politically provocative, and embarrassing to the King, as if, say, in our day the Prince of Wales suddenly announced that he had joined the Communist party and defiantly flaunted his membership card in public.

To accommodate his brother within the law and pour oil on the troubled waters, Charles therefore issued a royal proclamation on 15th March, 1672, called a *Declaration of Indulgence* which, on his own personal authority without reference to Parliament, suspended all penal laws discriminating against Roman Catholics and Protestant Non-Conformists. Thus a general religious toleration was allowed to all his subjects, not only to the Duke of York.

The Stuart kings firmly believed that, as Supreme Head of the Church of England, the right to issue such dispensations without reference to Parliament was inherent in their kingship—part of their divine right thus to exercise their royal prerogative, a right confirmed in Acts of Parliament—and many loyal subjects shared this belief.

The following year however Parliament retaliated by forcing the King to withdraw his personal Declaration of Indulgence, in return for an extra grant of £70,000 over three years, and promptly passed a contrary measure, the *Test Act*, which required all subjects holding public office under the Crown publicly to take the sacrament in the Church of England, and to renounce the controversial doctrine of transsubstantiation—the belief that the consecrated bread and water became the real body and blood of Christ.

Charles had perforce to give this Act his Royal Assent. All Catholics and Protestant Non-Conformists who refused to "take the Test" were thereby excluded from holding public office, including commissions in the army and navy.

The Duke of York, whose action in publicly joining the Church of Rome had provoked the measure, was forced to resign from his post as Lord High Admiral of the Fleet, a job which he enjoyed and had filled with some success.

In November 1673 James aroused further public disquiet by taking as his second wife the fifteen-year-old Italian Mary Beatrice d'Este—soon dubbed Mother East by the irreverent populace—daughter of the Duke of Modena, thus raising the spectre of a legitimate Catholic successor to the Throne after him.

Five years later, in 1678, a second *Test Act* excluded Catholics from sitting in the House of Commons.

In May 1679, when disquiet about the religion of the heir presumptive had reached fever heat, following the discovery of the Popish Plot,* the *first Exclusion Bill* was tabled in the House of Commons. It was designed expressly to debar James from acceding to the Throne because he was a Catholic. On 21st May it passed its Second Reading by 207 votes to 128, with 170 abstentions. But before it could come to Third Reading the King prorogued then dissolved Parliament.

To cool the issue, Charles banished his brother from Court and for three years, 1679 to 1682—with frequent hops back to London—James and his Italian Duchess lived well away from the capital, first in Brussels then in Edinburgh, where he acted as the King's commissioner in the Scottish Parliament and, despite all, was "well-esteemed" by the members.

Although a Test Act was passed there, similar to that of the English Parliament, which included promises to defend the King's prerogatives and adhere to the Protestant religion, another Act of 1681 guaranteed James's succession to the Scottish Crown.

---

*A bizarre rumour mischievously spread by Titus Oates that English Catholics, notably Jesuit priests, plotted with Louis XIV to kill Charles II, prevent the accession of James, then stage the conquest of England by Catholic France.

Mary of Modena in hunting costume. She was fifteen when she came to England in 1673 to marry the Duke of York, later James II, as his second wife, when he was forty. This lovely portrait by Verelst hangs at Windsor Castle.

James II by J. Riley c.1690. After William's landing he fled to France, thus forfeiting the Crown of three kingdoms.

In November 1680, during James's absence from London, a *second Exclusion Bill* passed all its three Readings in the House of Commons. One idea mooted during the debates on the Bill was that Princess Mary, James's elder daughter, now eighteen and heir presumptive after him, should jump the gun and occupy the Throne instead of her father when Charles II died. But the Bill was rejected by the House of Lords by 63 votes to 30.

Charles was thus spared the painful dilemma which would have confronted him, of having to choose between his brother and Parliament if the Bill had come to him for the Royal Assent. But he declared candidly that in any case he would never give the Royal Assent to any Bill which effectively disinherited James from his title to the Crown. Shining loyalty to his younger and politically awkward brother was one of Charles's more endearing characteristics.

The King was pressed on another raw nerve by the Protestant zealots of the Whig party to name his eldest illegitimate son, the Protestant Duke of Monmouth and Buccleuch, as his successor to the Crown in place of his Catholic brother.

Monmouth, a showy but rather weak character, was the hope and darling of the Protestant Whigs. He had a chip on his shoulder about his bastardy. He was haunted by the delusion that his Welsh mother, Lucy Walter, had indeed been married to his royal father before he was born in 1650, when Charles was nineteen, so he was not in fact illegitimate at all and was therefore the first heir to his father's Crown.

The more extreme Whigs fostered this delusion for their own political ends, to try to secure the Protestant succession to the Throne. They pressed the King to legitimise his son, "the Protestant Duke", whom they exploited as their figurehead and even deluded him into a tragic *folie de grandeur*, in actually thinking he was the rightful heir when his father died. But Charles resolutely refused to deny his brother's birthright in favour of one he knew to be his bastard son.

To put the matter beyond all doubt, the King wrote a disavowal in his own hand and signed it in the presence of some of his councillors, thus:

"For the avoyding of any dispute which may happen in time to come concerning the possession of the Crowne, I do heere declare in the presence of Almighty God, that I never gave nor made any contract of marriage, nor was married to any woman whatsoever, but to my present wife Queene Caterine (sic) now living. Whitehall the 3d day of March 1678/79   Charles R."*

Three months later, on 8th June, the document was published in the *London Gazette,* so there was no justification for any claim to legitimacy, and thus to the Crown, by Monmouth and his backers.

★　★　★　★

Four months after the defeat of the second Exclusion Bill by the House of Lords, Parliament met again at Oxford in March 1681, specifically to try to pass a *third Exclusion Bill* debarring James from acceding to the Throne. Many members attended with armed followers prepared to press their case at sword-point, but it did not come to that.

For Charles deftly countered this move by making a novel compromise proposal, that his nephew the Prince of Orange, Protestant champion of Europe and married to the Protestant Princess Mary, should be appointed Regent to carry on the government in James's name after his (Charles's) death.

This proposal was rejected however and the Commons voted for their third Exclusion Bill to be given a Second Reading. Charles's stock response was again effectively to kill the Bill by dissolving Parliament, which did not meet again for the rest of his reign.

His idea of Protestant William as a Regent for the Catholic King James, if and when the latter eventually succeeded to the Throne, had however been floated. Eight years later, as we shall see, when the country was in revolt against James, it was to be revived and strongly canvassed as an alternative to the distasteful and revolutionary act of renouncing allegiance to King James and transferring it to his Protestant daughter and Dutch—albeit half-Stuart—son-in-law.

For the rest of his reign Charles was constantly petitioned to call a new Parliament—which he carefully refused to do—expressly to get the Exclusion Bill on to the Statute Book and thus debar his Catholic brother from succeeding him on the Throne. But counter-petitions were also presented by those sympathetic to "the old religion" and the sanctity of the King's prerogative to rule as he thought fit, who "abhorred" the Bill.

*Quoted from *King Charles II* by Antonia Fraser.

The two factions, "Petitioners" and "Abhorrers", were nicknamed by their contemporaries "Whigs" and "Tories"; and, as the spiritual successors of the Roundheads and Cavaliers of the previous generation, they were the progenitors of our still basically two-party parliamentary system—radicals and conservatives.

The Whig epithet may have originated from some Scottish Protestant extremists called "Whiggamores", while Tory was a term of contempt used by Irish peasants.

CHAPTER SIX

The Declaration of Indulgence

Charles II died of a stroke on 6th February 1685 and James rejoiced in his accession to the Throne. Since the Exclusion Bill had not been enacted no one could seriously dispute it. At last he had the reins of government in his own hands to rule as *he* wanted; and now that he was King most people were prepared in good faith to work with him. After all, the Test Act was there as, it was thought, a defence against his possible excesses in filling public offices with Roman Catholics.

The King started all right at his first meeting of the Privy Council by assuring them that he would maintain the government of Church and State as by law established. But he had no real intention of doing so. Indeed, characteristically facing both ways, in a mixture of ingratiation and veiled threats, he told the Archbishop of Canterbury, William Sancroft, and the Bishop of London, Henry Compton,

> "I will keep my word and will undertake nothing against the religion established by law, assuming that you do your duty towards me. If you fail therein . . . I shall readily find the means of attaining my ends without your help."*

Secretly, his end was to make Britain into a one-party Roman Catholic state, overriding what he knew to be the Protestant majority in the country. He was to prove stupid, obstinate, misguided, autocratic and politically inept in his obsession to achieve this aim, and in the end

*Ranke, *History of England*, Vol. IV, p.219.

he failed miserably—although it must be added that he was neither bad nor wicked, nor was he lucky.

At his coronation on St. George's day, 23rd April, only ten weeks after his brother's death, James took the oath in accordance with the ancient rituals; but, since he was not of the Anglican communion, the sacrament was omitted. In retrospect, this marked a fatal defect in the spiritual commitment of his kingship.

Afterwards a lavish coronation banquet, personally organised by the King himself, was held in Westminster Hall, at which he took a schoolboy pleasure in seeing the peers and peeresses in their coronets and ermine serve him and his Italian Catholic Queen on bended knee. They had all taken the oath of allegiance to their new Sovereign. Yet in less than four years most would reluctantly but unreservedly renounce that allegiance in favour of new oaths to James's daughter Mary and her Anglo-Dutch husband, the Prince of Orange.

James II's Coronation banquet in Westminster Hall. The three horsemen in the centre are the King's Champion, flanked by the Earl Marshal and the Lord High Constable. Besides "Hot Meat" being served here, guests were also regaled on soused carps, pickled oysters and periwinkles, trotter pie and cold bamboo pudding.

The Duke of Monmouth, who had been exiled to Holland by his father for his embarrassing pretensions, now put his oar in. In a foolhardy exploit which, given his unsuitability as a leader and the weakness of his claim, never had a chance of succeeding, he attempted to seize the Crown from his uncle.

Hastening home from Holland, having loaded four ships with arms and ammunition, he landed at Lyme Regis in Dorset on 11th June with about eighty extremist followers. They proceeded to Taunton in Somerset where, on 20th June, he issued a Declaration and proclaimed himself King Monmouth. His own name being also James, this distinguished him from the new King.

This was rebellion, rank and brazen. The King immediately dispatched the royal army to the West country and defeated the rebels in a rout at the battle of Sedgemoor on 6th July. Monmouth escaped, disguised in peasant's garb, and made for the south coast. But, with £50,000 on his head, he was betrayed and captured while hiding in a ditch in the New Forest.

Taken back to London on horseback with his hands tied behind his back, he was summarily executed without trial on Tower Hill on 15th July. His head was sewn back on his body, which was then buried under the altar in the chapel of St. Peter ad Vincula within the precincts of the Tower.

For this ill-conceived rising the West country was cruelly and excessively punished by the notoriously savage Lord Chancellor Jeffreys, presiding personally over what came to be known as the Bloody Assizes. Three hundred poor peasant souls were hanged, and eight hundred and forty-one transported to the West Indies in terrible shipboard conditions. That summer the roads in the West country were disfigured by gibbets swinging with tattered corpses.

On 2nd May, 1685, a month earlier than Monmouth, the exiled Earl of Argyll had likewise slipped away from Holland out of the Zuyder Zee, with three ships laden with arms, ammunition and a few tatterdemalion supporters, to stage a similar rebellion against King James in his northern kingdom.

Sailing via the north and west coast of Scotland, he landed at a remote spot near Campbeltown at the southern tip of his ancestral fiefdom of Argyllshire, and thence up the Clyde to Greenock. But his rebellion in Scotland, intended to double with that of Monmouth in England, likewise drew no more than indifferent peasant support. It likewise ended in failure with the execution of Argyll on the Edinburgh guillotine on 30th June, less than two months after his landing in Scotland.

★ ★ ★ ★

As King, James soon showed his true colours by a series of arbitrary or illegal acts which increasingly outraged and exasperated both politicians and people, and the clergy.

1. He appointed Roman Catholics illegally to public office, and to commissions in the armed forces, in defiance of the Test Act. He claimed, justifiably enough, that, by virtue of his royal prerogative under Divine right, he had power to dispense with a law if he so wished; but he wrongly used this "dispensing power", as it was called, to nullify the Test Act without reference to Parliament. He appointed judges who would rule that this use by the King of the dispensing power was legal.

2. He interfered with the freedom of the universities by putting up his own Catholic nominee, a drunkard and debaucher, Anthony Farmer, sacked from Trinity at Cambridge, as president of Magdalen College, Oxford. When the twenty-five Fellows of Magdalen refused to vote for his man and elected their own choice, Dr. Hough, James flew into a rage and ordered his second nominee Samuel Parker, Bishop of Oxford, to break open the door of the college and forcibly take over the presidency. The Fellows were then summarily expelled at sword-point and replaced with papists.

    This episode is depicted on a mural in the Peers Corridor of the Houses of Parliament.

3. In July 1687 he received in public audience at St. James's Palace, actually sinking to his knees, a Papal Nuncio or envoy from the Pope, Cardinal d'Adda, outraging public opinion. Papal envoys had not been officially received in London since the Reformation. When the Duke of Somerset, Lord of the Bedchamber, refused to attend, the King instantly "turned him out of all his employments in the Household and army with expressions of high displeasure."*

*Burnet.

4. He tried to pack the House of Commons with papists, by revoking town and city charters, including that of the City of London, unless they returned Catholic members to Parliament.

5. He likewise ordered the Lords Lieutenant of the counties to submit to him a list of Catholics and Non-Conformists to stand as sole candidates for election to Parliament in their respective shires, thereby excluding Anglicans from standing. Many of these local dignitaries evaded compliance with this royal edict by promptly resigning their offices.

By such high-handed and arbitrary tactics, actually boasting in so many words that as King he was above the law, James sought to obtain a puppet Parliament packed with Roman Catholic or non-Anglican members subservient to his will, thus forcing England into a one-party papist State—notwithstanding that the Catholic minority in the country represented only about two per cent of the total population.

9. In July 1686 he created a *Court of High Commission,* also called the *Ecclesiastical Commission,* a kind of kangaroo court, "as a prevention of indiscreet preaching upon controversial points", that is, to arraign and gag the clergy from opposing his pro-papist policies—the pulpits being then the main medium of communication between government and people—thus infringing freedom of speech to silence criticism of his actions. As he openly boasted to the French Ambassador, "It will give me the right to exercise a power still greater than that of Catholic kings in other European countries."

All European kings in those days were absolute monarchs; there was no such thing as a democracy, royal or otherwise.

The Archbishop of Canterbury refused to serve on the Ecclesiastical Commission. One of its first acts was to suspend the Bishop of London, Henry Compton, from his duties, thus antagonising him permanently against the King—we will hear more of him later.

That same month, to show he meant business, James camped his swollen army of 13,000 men, many of them Irish papists, just outside London on Hounslow Heath—now Heathrow airport—purposely to intimidate his subjects. He even trundled a mobile altar there to celebrate Mass publicly and provocatively in the camp.

10. In April 1687 the King went further. He issued by royal proclamation a *Declaration of Indulgence* which, he claimed, empowered him to suspend on his own personal authority the Test Act, which excluded Catholics and Protestant Non-Conformists from public office. He then appointed four Roman Catholics to his Privy Council.

This naturally increased public resentment and alarm. It was seen as a further tightening of the screw to force England into a one-party Catholic dictatorship, subservient to the Pope and Louis XIV.

On top of all this James offended people by ostentatiously celebrating Mass in public, by establishing new Roman Catholic chapels, and by opening for public celebration of Roman rituals the Chapel Royal at St. James's Palace, which he had allotted to his Catholic Queen as her "private oratory".

The Queen's numerous foreign papist attendants were suspected of harbouring a nest of French spies and popish agents. Evelyn indeed saw with alarm, shared by the country in general, "Romanists swarming at Court with greater confidence than had ever yet been seen in England since the Reformation."*

In 1672 Charles II, as we have seen, had also issued a Declaration of Indulgence which likewise suspended the penal laws against Catholics and Protestant Dissenters, as Non-Conformists were then called. But, more sensible and politically astute than his brother, he had withdrawn it the following year under pressure from Parliament.

Charles always knew how far he could go, and stopped short of a head-on clash with his Parliaments.

But James obstinately ignored or dissolved any Parliament which opposed his rulings. It is reckoned that he violated the laws and endeavoured to extirpate Protestantism and the liberties of his subjects in thirteen particular instances.**

Few people actually denied the right of the King to hold and exercise the dispensing and suspending power as he might think fit—it was part of his royal prerogative. It was the extreme use to which James put these powers, to silence criticism of his pro-Catholic policies, which aroused misgivings then opposition.

---

*Evelyn's Diary, 2nd October, 1685.
**The Declaration of Rights 1689 by Lois G. Schwoerer.

The distinction between the dispensing and suspending power was a fine one. The former meant to dispense with a law in particular and individual instances, and had to be applied for personally and granted by royal warrant through a magistrate. The latter meant temporarily to stop the operation of a law in a general sense, without actually repealing it by another Act of Parliament.

What was really at issue under James II, and opposed by most people, was not the right of the King to use the dispensing and suspending power, but the way in which this right was exercised by James in favour of Catholics.

The Queen's Pardon, issued nowadays on her behalf by the Home Secretary for a civil misdemeanour on which a conviction has been made, is a way in which the dispensing power is still exercised by the Sovereign.

CHAPTER SEVEN

The Seven Bishops

A year later James pushed his luck even further, indeed too far. He brought the general discontent to the boil on 4th May, 1688, by ordering the clergy to read his *Declaration of Indulgence* from every pulpit in the land at their Sunday services on 20th May and 27th May following. This the majority of them refused to do.

The Archbishop of Canterbury and six other bishops* demurred, but tactfully did not refuse point blank to obey the King's order. Instead, after a meeting at Lambeth Palace, they jointly presented a petition to James in carefully chosen respectful terms, requesting to be excused from reading the royal decree to their flocks because, arbitrarily dispensing as it did with the law—the *Test Act*—it was illegal, and they could not be party to an illegal act.

James's furious answer was to seize the seven men of God and clap them into the Tower on a trumped-up charge of "seditious libel". They were later released on bail to await trial.

---

*The Seven were the Archbishop of Canterbury, Lloyd of St. Asaph, Turner of Ely, Lake of Chichester, Ken of Bath and Wells, White of Peterborough, and Trelawney of Bristol.

Seven vicars in London and about two hundred throughout the country did read the King's Declaration with various individual reservations and qualifications. One incumbent ingeniously solved his dilemma by telling his congregation that, although the King's command obliged him to read the Declaration, they were not obliged to listen to it, so "when they had all gone out he read it to the walls."*

At this precise juncture, in the midst of the public turmoil at the tightening of the royal dictatorship, the Queen was delivered of a son, providing on the face of it a legitimate heir apparent to the Throne. The birth threw an entirely new and unexpected factor into the now boilding cauldron of public affairs.

The Seven Bishops were duly brought to trial on 29th June. Next day, after the jury had been out all night, a verdict of "not guilty" was returned, and the accused were all acquitted.

This result was greeted by a spontaneous explosion of joy from the London populace, echoed out to the west by the still mainly Protestant soldiers encamped on Hounslow Heath; in pointed contrast to the stony silence, and indeed scornful disbelief, occasioned by the birth of the Prince of Wales three weeks before.

James however, far from noting the ominous thunder claps of public discontent, bone-headedly refused to admit the popular challenge to his authority as it was, and temper the wind to the shorn lamb. He even petulantly and pettily ordered that those humble subjects who had lit bonfires to celebrate the Bishops' acquittal should be prosecuted. But when the accused came to court, the juries found no case to answer.

CHAPTER EIGHT

The Cause of Revolution: Birth of a Prince of Wales

The direct cause of the Glorious Revolution, however, was not James's "bad acts" but the birth of the baby Prince. Although exasperated by the King's Catholic extremism and dictatorial personal rule in pursuit of it, the lieges were nonetheless prepared to tolerate him for his lifetime—and he was already fifty-five—because on his death the Crown

*Burnet.

would pass to his elder daughter the Princess Mary, a staunch Protestant as already noted, and married to the Protestant Prince of Orange.

So ultimately the undisputed Protestant ascendancy in the kingdom, with basically common ground between Sovereign, Parliament and People, seemed assured.

William was indeed doubly eligible, being himself a Stuart of the blood royal through his mother, also Princess Mary, daughter of Charles I, and third in line for the Throne in his own right after his wife and her sister the Princess Anne, both of whom were at that date childless.

But at ten o'clock on that fateful morning of 10th June, 1688, the young Queen, James's second wife the Italian Mary of Modena—whom he had married in 1673 when she was only fifteen and he was forty—unexpectedly produced a living son and heir after fifteen years of as yet unfruitful marriage.

The country was thunderstruck. The birth was universally believed to be a Catholic hoax. "The Queen's bigness" was ascribed to obesity not pregnancy, and anyway she was rumoured to have miscarried in April. Having had at least four miscarriages and lost another four babies in infancy, with no evident pregnancy for the past five years, a living male heir for James was no longer reckoned with on the political spectrum.

So the news of the birth at St. James's Palace, where the Queen had been hustled the previous night under cover of darkness from Whitehall by Charing Cross and Pall Mall, was received with disbelief and consternation amounting to panic.

It was a malign stroke of fate which dashed to nought the hopes of a Protestant succession. For the new prince would be raised as a bigoted Roman Catholic like his father, so an endless succession of Catholic Stuart kings, all claiming a Divine right to rule in defiance of Parliament, stretched nightmarishly before the good people of Britain, it seemed for ever.

From the highest to the lowest in the land people refused to believe, because they did not want to believe, that the birth was genuine. It was faked to procure a Catholic succession—an old trick. A changling had been smuggled into the Queen's bed in a warming pan. A cruel Dutch cartoon showed her pinning on a cushion to imply a false pregnancy; even though the Prince of Orange, at first unaware of the public disbelief in England and much to his wife's annoyance, had sent James a congratulatory message and ordered prayers for her new half-brother to be said in the Princess's private chapel at the Hague, to which however she did not object.

Exactly nine months before, in September 1687, James and his Queen had admittedly spent a week together at Bath. But James had gone to Chester to meet the Earl of Tyrconnel, his Catholic governor in Ireland, and had then made a trip alone to the shrine of St. Winifred at Holywell in North Wales. It had long been closed, but he ordered it to be unsealed and prayed there on bended knee for a son. This merely fuelled the suspicion that the birth was contrived to provide the required Divine answer to the prayer. It all looked too coincidental.

With his usual indifference to public opinion, James did nothing to dispel the suspicions concerning the birth—indeed he fanned them. Although he had invited sixty-seven witnesses—courtiers and foreign envoys—to attend the confinement, no representative of Princess Mary or Princess Anne was summoned, although the newcomer, if male, would obviously displace them in the succession. Indeed, Princess Anne had been spirited away on holiday to Bath with Sara Churchill in that very week.

The crush of people in the bedchamber had been kept at the other end of the room, with the ladies—more knowledgeable in these matters—pushed into an alcove, and the Queen had asked for the curtains to be drawn round the bed, to screen her from so many staring male eyes.

Natural enough, one might think, but in the circumstances all adding to the suspicions. A warming pan was seen being hurried behind the drapes and a bundle carried as shiftily out to an adjacent room. No slap, or cry from the new-born, was heard; and the more unsavoury signs of childbirth had flaws which fed the gossip, all retailed in salacious detail by letters from Princess Anne to her sister at the Hague. From birth the baby was branded as a pretender, and if not at birth then he was substituted for a dead royal infant soon after.

The Parliamentarians resolved to act. In stately homes and cellars all over the country the local gentry went into huddles, surreptitiously whispering rebellion. The seven top conspirators met secretly to hatch the master plot, probably in the London house of the Earl of Shrewsbury. A letter was written by them to William of Orange inviting, indeed imploring him to bring an army over to oust James and secure the Protestant religion and a free Parliament.

It was signed in cipher by the seven plotters who hid their identity behind numbers instead of appending their signatures—the earls of Shrewsbury, Devonshire and Danby, Henry Sidney (who penned the letter), Lord Lumley, Lord Edward Russell and Henry Compton, the suspended Bishop of London—the Immortal Seven as they were later styled.

Their heads were now well and truly on the line. The letter was high treason. It was carried secretly down the Thames to the Hague by Admiral Herbert disguised as a common seaman. He hid it under his vest. He nursed a personal grudge, the King having replaced him as Lord High Admiral of the Fleet by Lord Dartmouth.

The letter assured William that he would be welcomed by ninety-five per cent of the people, who were exasperated with James's Romanising zeal and believed that the birth of the Prince of Wales was faked. Even the officers in James's army were wavering in their loyalty to him, and the common soldiers were solidly anti-popery. Now was the time to act before the King could pack Parliament and the armed forces, as was his intention, with Catholics, to fix his popish dictatorship on the nation.

William was urged to make the alleged hoax birth of a papist heir to the Throne the justification for a military descent on England. Already in any case his army included three English and three Scottish regiments stationed on permanent friendly loan at the Hague to help defend Holland against Louis XIV. The signatories expected the Prince to bring all necessary armament and ammunition, and "some good engineers", by which they probably meant what we would now call artificers and blacksmiths.

The letter did not come as a surprise to William. Admiral Herbert, under cover of visiting his sister in Holland, and Lord Russell, and the Dutch envoy to England, Zulestein, had been busily commuting back and forth across the North Sea to the Hague since April, with messages indicating the disquiet of many public men at James's misconduct of affairs, and hints of support for William as regent in his place. The Prince had responded to these feelers in fairly positive terms thus:

"If he was invited by some men of the best interest . . . [i.e. of sufficient standing] to come and rescue the [British] nation and the [Protestant] religion he believed he could be ready by the end of September to come over."*

*Sir John Dalrymple, *Memoirs of Great Britain and Ireland.* 2 Vols. London 1771-73.

So the specific request of 30th June was not a bolt from the blue. It was taken more as a confirmation that events had come to a head and the time was ripe.

William replied in a lengthy Declaration to the British people

"of the Reasons Inducing him to Appear in Armes in the Kingdom of England for Preserving of the Protestant Religion and for Restoring the Lawes and Liberties of England, Scotland and Ireland."*

It was circulated in the Hague in July but not issued in London until 30th September. It listed James's illegal acts, and the belief that the birth of the Prince of Wales was a hoax; that, as the husband of Princess Mary, the King's daughter and hitherto his heiress presumptive, he would come with an army, not as a conqueror but as a Deliverer, to secure the Protestant religion and a free and legal Parliament, by whose decisions he would abide.

A top Dutchman, the Grand Pensionary Fagel, assisted by Lord Danby, advised William in the drafting of his Declaration, and it was translated for the British public into easily readable English by Bishop Gilbert Burnet, chaplain to the Princess of Orange. This practical Scotsman (1643-1715) had sought refuge in Holland in May 1686 when his anti-papist preaching had laid him open to the risk of imprisonment by James.

The Prince's *Declaration of Reasons* was published in English, Dutch, German and French. It was printed in the Hague, Amsterdam, Edinburgh, Hamburg, London, Magdeburg, Rotterdam and York. Copies were issued to all ambassadors at the Hague. It was widely distributed in Europe, but of course only clandestinely in Britain.

The effort made by William to ensure the general Continent-wide knowledge of his Declaration shows that he considered his military expedition to England to be in the interests of Protestant Europe and the balance of power in general, not just a local bid for the British Crown in pursuit of his own personal aggrandisement.

A password "I come from Exeter" was used to assure William's friends in England that the man slipping them a copy of the Declaration under the table in a coffee house was a genuine supporter of the Prince and not a government plant to trap them into a charge of sedition.

The Declaration of Rights 1689 by Lois B. Schwoerer.

CHAPTER NINE

William's Position

The immediate result of the receipt by William of the conspirators' invitation was that prayers for the baby Prince, which had been much resented in England, ceased to be said in the Princess's private chapel at the Hague.

But William's position was delicate, to say the least.

As Stadtholder, an ancient provincial title roughly equivalent to hereditary president or head of the Dutch Netherlands—then called the United Provinces*—he was secretly invited by seven English conspirators, out of favour with their own government with whom he was in friendly if increasingly strained relations, to attempt a *coup d'état* in England similar to that of the Duke of Monmouth which had so disastrously failed only three years before to usurp the Crown from James.

To achieve this difficult feat he was asked to mount a major sea-borne expedition and land in England with an army of foreigners to confront the British army on its home ground, with the support of "ninety-five per cent" of the population and "some men of the best interest" expected but not assured—how the cat would jump on his actual landing was the sixty-four thousand dollar question.

He had to obtain the approval, by no means certain, for his adventure from his own "federal parliament", the States-General; some of whom, including the key port of Amsterdam, were hostile to the House of Orange and friendly towards Louis XIV of France, William's chief rival on the Continent and likely to try to thwart his invasion of England.

In staging an attempted *coup* against his papist uncle-cum-father-in-law, he did not want thereby to provoke the enmity of the Pope and the Catholic Great Powers of Europe, because he needed their tacit support to preserve the balance of power and prevent Louis XIV from conquering Holland, and ultimately achieving the overlordship of Europe for France.

Last but not least, he had to make all the preparations for a

---

*A federation of seven provinces—Holland, Zeeland, Utrecht, Guelderland, Overissel, Friesland and Groningen.

substantial sea-borne military expedition *without arousing the suspicions of James and Louis, and even of his own States-General.*

William saw clearly that he had to keep all these moving balls in the air simultaneously, and get his act right the first time. One fudged decision, one misjudgement or mishandling or mis-timing, could topple the whole design, and there would be no second chance.

A master of men's minds, and of his own, William waited and watched. Like Brer Rabbit he just lay low and said nothing. He did not wait and watch for long, or in vain.

While James was busy creating among his most loyal subjects the resentments and despair which forced them into rebellion against him in William's favour, the King's patron and ally and William's main adversary, Louis XIV of France, was likewise as perversely shooting himself in the foot by making major political blunders which not only put him out of the contest that summer, but positively redounded to William's advantage.

Birth of the Prince of Wales at St. James's Palace on 10th June, 1688, which sparked off the Revolution. It was said that the birth was faked to procure a Catholic heir to the Throne by smuggling a changling into the Queen's bed in a warming pan.

The Dutch Netherlands in 1688.

—— *Frontier of the Republic of Dutch United Provinces. Holland was the principal state of a federation of seven provinces or states ruled by the States-General.*

CHAPTER TEN

James's Folly and Louis's Vanity

Thus, in the event William's passage in the autumn of 1688 was almost miraculously opened and smoothed by the folly of James and the mistakes of Louis XIV.

There were four issues over which the French king unexpectedly alienated those of his friends who might otherwise have helped him to thwart or at least hinder William's expedition to England. They can be listed as: 1. Huguenots; 2. Herrings; 3. Ambassadorial enclaves; and 4. The archbishopric of Cologne.

1. A sizeable minority, about one million, of Huguenots, or French Protestants, many of Dutch descent, had been settled in France for nearly a hundred years since the Reformation, peaceably to ply their trades as skilled artisans. As much as Catholic Frenchmen they were Louis's loyal subjects. They had been protected for almost a century by the *Edict of Nantes* (1598) of Henri IV of France, which allowed them freely to practise their own religion in a Roman Catholic country.

In 1685 however, Louis XIV needlessly revoked his grandfather's Edict, thus exposing the Huguenots to persecution and massacre by the French Catholic mobs. Some 200,000 fled their country in droves, an estimated 50,000 seeking asylum in England, there to become with their skills a hard core of enmity towards France.

2. A lucrative trade in the export of herrings and manufactured goods from Holland to France was needlessly banned by Louis in gross breach of a trading agreement, thus alienating at a stroke the merchants of Amsterdam who, with a weather eye for business, had until then been friendly towards France.

The ban on their imports to France however, turned them with their money from opponents into warm supporters of the House of Orange, with whom they had hitherto been in a state of feud. But for this needless provocation by Louis, the key city of Amsterdam with its port could and possibly would have tried to prevent William's fleet from leaving Holland, thereby aborting or at least hamstringing the *coup* at its start.

3. A relatively trivial matter of etiquette was needlessly blown up by Louis's vanity into a bitter quarrel with the Vatican.

The independent status and diplomatic immunities of foreign ambassadorial enclaves in Rome had made them into safe havens for spies and criminals. That very summer of 1688 these privileges were of necessity abolished by Pope Innocent XI; but Louis XIV, the Most Christian King, was the only Head of State who refused to accept the papal decree.

The French ambassador to Italy was ordered by his master to flaunt this refusal by ostentatiously marching to his palace in the ambassadorial enclave in Rome escorted by soldiers to assert, in splendid isolation from the other embassies in the city, diplomatic immunity for the French.

Having thus alienated one great Protestant branch of Christendom by persecuting the Huguenots, Louis then antagonised the Catholic branch by insulting the Holy See.

4. The important archbishopric of Cologne, a semi-secular province which governed the strategically vital middle Rhine valley and bordered the south-eastern frontier of the United Provinces, happened to become vacant in that fateful midsummer of 1688, and Louis further antagonised the Vatican by pushing his nominee for the vacancy against the nominee of the Pope. He even backed his nominee with force, by sending French troops into the Rhineland—then called the Palatinate— burning the farms and harassing the local peasants, who were predominantly inoffensive Lutheran Protestants.

French arms and attention were thus diverted from northern France and Flanders away into central Europe at the precise moment when the English Channel should have been watched for William's fleet. In time of war the Archbishop of Cologne could put 20,000 men into the field, so Louis had to divert an equivalent number of French troops into the Rhineland to fight the minor war he had himself started backstage while the main action determining the future of Great Britain, and the balance of power in Europe, was unfolding at the front on the western Continental seaboard.

In 1688 the principality of Orange, from which the Princes of Orange took their hereditary title, was not remotely connected geographically with the Netherlands. It was a small Protestant enclave in the south of France, centred on the town of Orange near Avignon in Provence. Not surprisingly, Louis XIV resented its existence in the heart of his

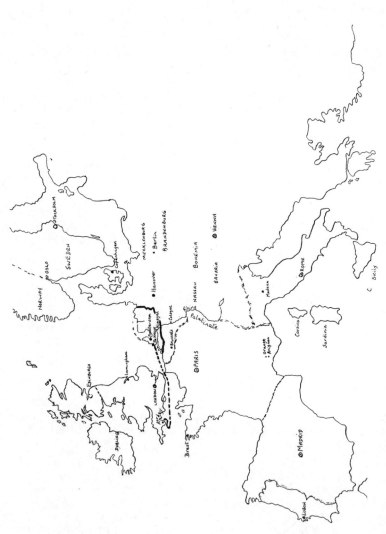

Europe in the late 17th Century showing William's voyage from Helvoetslys to Torbay. It also shows how small the Dutch United Provinces were in relation to the other European Powers.

Catholic kingdom, providing as it did a haven for political discontents and Huguenot refugees.

In 1660, taking advantage of the minority of the Prince of Orange, then aged nine, Louis had bribed the Dutch governor to surrender it to the French. The seizure was deeply resented by William's mother, who was nevertheless forced to accept the appointment of a Roman Catholic governor.

William never forgave Louis XIV for this annexation of his hereditary principality. It was restored to the Prince by the Treaty of Nimegen in 1678, but re-taken by Louis in 1682 when the fortifications were razed to the ground. It was finally incorporated with France under the Treaty of Utrecht in 1713, but the town of Orange still of course remains.

CHAPTER ELEVEN

Louis XIV Offers Help to James II

At the end of August Louis momentarily left his war games to play realpolitik. He instructed the French ambassador to the Hague, Avaux, to warn the States-General that he had taken James under his protection, and that an attack on England by William would be considered as a declaration of war on France.

This protection was to be effected by a loan of sixteen French warships. But the offer was petulantly rejected by James who, at the precise moment when he needed his cousin's help, refused in a fit of false pride to be in hock to him. The English ambassador to France, Sir Bevil Skelton, who had skilfully manipulated Louis into making the offer, was recalled by James and clapped into the Tower for his pains.

Louis also promised James enough French troops, if needed, to "subdue his enemies"—i.e. to enforce Catholicism on his mainly Protestant English subjects.

In contrast, the Dutch ambassador to London, Van Citters, was warmly received by the King at St. James's Palace to convey his master's assurance that William was not contemplating an invasion of England. Certainly the States-General had not yet sanctioned an expedition, and might not do so; but, although all the signs indicated that the Dutchman spoke with his tongue in his cheek, James took him at face value and believed him.

Peeved by James's snub in rejecting his offer of ships and soldiers, Louis then withdrew the French troops which threatened the Dutch frontier in Flanders—where they had been posted to stiffen his warning to William not to mount a descent upon England—and poured them, three separate armies strong, into the Middle Rhine from Baden to Bonn—scoring a triumphant but irrelevant victory at Philipsburg en route—to reinforce his fight there over the trumped-up issue of the election of the new Archbishop of Cologne, quite inconsequential though it was to the main struggle in western Europe.

So, sitting tight at the Hague, and without any word or action on his part, William saw the French armies which menaced his frontier if he embarked for England conveniently removed out of his way, like a misdirected missile, into central Europe; and the sixteen French warships, which could have impeded the passage of his invasion fleet to England, rejected by James.

The net result of this posturing by the vainglorious King of France was that William was able to conceal the considerable military preparations for his expedition under the plausible pretext that they were intended to contest or contain Louis's aggression in the Middle Rhine.

In particular, it gave the Prince an excuse for assembling the three hundred supply ships essential for his invasion of England. They were loaded inland at Nimegen pretendedly as if ready to move up the Rhine should action against Louis around Cologne be required.

CHAPTER TWELVE

James Awakes to his Danger

The publication of William's Declaration at the Hague in July, as reported to James, annoyed but did not alarm him, and did not deter him from pursuing his pro-Catholic policies. With his head firmly in the sand, it was unthinkable to him that William, his nephew and son-in-law, with whom he had formerly until his accession to the Throne been on good terms, would or indeed could mount from overseas an invasion of his kingdom to usurp his Crown.

Not until 21st August did the King wake up to the reality that William might seriously be planning an expedition to England; and he ordered the preparation of an extra thirty-five ships, including fire-ships, in the Thames estuary to augment his thirty warships at Sheerness.

On 24th August, by now bestirred out of his complacency and really alarmed by the prospect of a Dutch invasion, James announced that he would call a new Parliament for 27th November. But this was only a sop to buy off the parliamentary wolves—he had no intention of doing so, and in fact he cancelled the writs of 21st September when he heard on the seventeenth that William's expected sailing from Holland had been prevented by contrary winds.

Throughout the crisis indeed, James blew hot and cold over his use of this instrument of royal power. He glibly promised to call a Parliament when things seemed to be going against him, and as capriciously went back on his word and cancelled the writs if his prospects seemed to improve. But his central aim and lodestar remained constant—to make Britain into a one-party Roman Catholic state with himself as its absolute monarch or arbitrary ruler.

William's sailing had only been postponed, not cancelled. Galvanised into action at last, James began tardily to mobilise his forces and ordered the army officers to stand by. His regular army of 13,000 men was the largest that any King of England had ever commanded. Nevertheless he rapidly enlarged it by recruiting another 4,000 men in England, 3,000 from Scotland, and 3,000 from Ireland, the latter of course all papists.

His forces finally totalled nearly 40,000, not counting the militia or "trained bands" as they were then called. However, many were so ill-equipped that they existed only on paper, and at least 2,500 were servants or otherwise untrained rabble and non-combatants. The effective strength was probably about 25,000, ten thousand more than that of William.

But the will to fight in the royal soldiers and seamen was doubtful, and the continuing loyalty of the officers was strained. James's idea of overpacking the army with Irish papists had reached the point where he could thereby forfeit the loyalty of the main body of predominantly Protestant and anti-papist troops. Some officers indeed flatly refused to take any more Irishmen into their ranks.

Forced to face the alarming fact that William meant business, James now reversed his refusal to accept French naval assistance, and asked Louis XIV for the sixteen warships he had offered in June to be kept in readiness at Brest, for use if they were needed. But, having been snubbed once, Louis said it was too late in the season to move them into the Channel area from the Mediterranean. Another unmentioned reason was that the exodus of Huguenots from France had left him short of seamen to man his ships.

Thus, in the event, not a hostile French sail stood forth from their Channel coast to dispute the passage of William's fleet through the Strait of Dover a few weeks later. The royal navy, trapped when the time came by a strong east wind in the Thames estuary, was likewise powerless to intercept.

A strange psychological factor now brought a subtle influence to bear on events. People everywhere sang and whistled a meaningless piece of anti-papist doggerel called "Lillibullero", set to a catchy tune by Henry Purcell, organist at Westminster Abbey.

It caught on like wildfire, for the tune not the inane words, rather like "She'll be coming round the mountain when she comes." Its influence, out of all proportion to its importance, was such that it was said to have "whistled King James out of three kingdoms."

Another new song was sung at this time—it is now one of our best known nursery rhymes.

Rock-a-bye baby, on the tree top,
When the wind blows, the cradle will rock,
When the bough breaks, the cradle will fall,
Down will come baby, cradle and all.

The baby was of course the King's newly-born son, and the wind was the easterly which would bring the Prince of Orange over to England.

With the crisis mounting daily, and despite the public chagrin at the unacceptable birth of the Prince of Wales, James nevertheless with supreme tactlessness had the baby christened on 15th October at St. James's Palace into the Church of Rome—with the Pope and the Catholic Dowager Queen Catherine as godparents!

A week later the King summoned all the lords spiritual and temporal in town—fifty-four—to hear forty witnesses testify, in every indelicate detail, that the birth of his son was genuine. The evidence was irrefutable and accepted by the embarrassed company.

But it was too late—the die was cast and events were already moving on their irresistible course.

CHAPTER THIRTEEN

The Princess of Orange

During that crisis summer the position of the Princess Mary, both as a woman and as a State personage, was as delicate as it was important. Her modesty and self-effacing nature, although negative virtues, were no small factor in contributing to the success of William's *coup*. Although she never demanded it, she earned her place ultimately as joint Sovereign with him and Queen Regnant in her own right.

Born in 1662, the elder of the two daughters of James II in a shotgun marriage to his first wife Anne Hyde, Mary was the granddaughter of the High Tory Cavalier Chancellor, Edward Hyde, Earl of Clarendon.

When she was twelve James planned with Louis XIV to marry her to his son, the Dauphin of France, but this scheme was frustrated by the general desire in Britain to see the heiress-presumptive to the Throne "sleep in Protestant arms". Her first cousin, William, Prince of Orange, offered his arms, and the arranged marriage—which produced floods of tears from the Princess when she was told of her fate—took place in 1677 when she was fifteen and he was twenty-seven. Despite three miscarriages it was happy, but she remained childless.

Her confidence in and devotion to her husband were complete. She had no scruples of conscience about her loyalty to him being paramount over her filial duty to her father, from whom, after eleven years of separation since her marriage, she had become estranged. It rankled with her that he had never paid her, his heiress-presumptive, her dowry, although he allowed her younger sister, Princess Anne, married to Prince George of Denmark, £20,000 a year. James's only interest in his elder daughter was to suspect her of influencing William against him, and he infiltrated her household with his spies and agents.

Mary was sweet-natured, devout and domesticated, absorbed in her religion and her Dutch houses and gardens—Hampton Court and Kensington Palace are her monuments in England. But, after nine years of marriage, William brooded over a secret worry which stultified their relationship. If, in pursuit of her interest, he succeeded in displacing her father from the Throne, would she insist on being Queen Regnant thereafter, leaving him to play a secondary role only as her Consort, her "gentleman usher"—a position he could not and would not accept.

William, Prince of Orange, aged 27. Portrait by Lely painted in 1677 in London at the time of his wedding to Princess Mary, elder daughter of James, Duke of York. When Wissing painted the Prince for James II in 1685, as a companion portrait to that of Princess Mary, he copied exactly this fine Lely pose with the same armour.

Mary, Princess of Orange, after a portrait by W. Wissing commissioned by her father in 1685 when she became his heir-presumptive on his accession to the Throne. In the original painting a prayer-book is shown in the space occupied in this later copy by the Crown.

William confided his concern over this matter to Bishop Burnet, the Princess's chaplain and mentor. Burnet told his mistress, who unreservedly assured him that she was no feminist, she had always regarded her husband as her superior in all matters of State; and, if and when they were established in Whitehall, she would never accept a position which left him subordinate to her.

The Bishop hurried back to reassure William on this point; and from then on the relationship of the Prince and Princess was one of serene mutual confidence and respect, unclouded by competition.

Later she proved herself a competent Queen Regnant during William's frequent absences abroad in Holland and Ireland. Her death from smallpox at Christmas 1694, aged only thirty-two, left him prostrated with grief, a lonely and desolate widower until his own death in 1702.

CHAPTER FOURTEEN

William Sails for England

Since receiving the invitation to bring an expedition to England, William had quietly mobilised 9,000 foot soldiers and 4,000 cavalrymen with their horses, plus 9,000 seamen. His troops were encamped for two months near the three hundred supply ships up the Rhine at Nimegen, ostensibly to cover Louis's sabre-rattling at Cologne.

Early in October they boarded the transports assembled in the Zuyder Zee, where they lay for ten days waiting for the wind to change into the east. But by then they had consumed so much of their provisions that three days of the good easterly were lost while these were replenished.

On 16th October William took leave of his States-General at the Hague. Many of the members were in tears at the departure of their beloved Stadtholder on so risky an adventure so unpredictable in its outcome. The Prince had prudently arranged with his cousin the Elector of Brandenburg and the Dukes of Hesse and Lunenburg that, with the removal of so many Dutch soldiers to England, the defence of the Dutch Republic against France would be covered in their absence by an adequate strength of his neighbours' forces.

On 19th October the Prince boarded the *Brill*, the new 28-gun flagship of the Admiral of Rotterdam, at Helvoetslys in the mouth of the Maas, just south of the Hague. Among those who accompanied him on board were the Earl of Shrewsbury, Lord Edward Russell, Henry Sidney and Bishop Burnet. He had appointed the latter as his chaplain for the expedition. The two former had gone over to the Hague in September with the latest news from the conspirators and £12,000 in cash. Indeed, a shuttle service of fast flyboats operated secretly all that summer between eastern England and the Hague.

The Dutch fleet comprised fifty warships and twenty-six frigates, eighteen fire-ships and three hundred transports and supply ships, plus an extra hundred "Schievelingers", or Dutch fishing boats with their crews, requisitioned at the last moment for extra stores. Besides the ordinary provisions, and saddles and harness for 4,000 horses, and small arms, room was found for 4 tons of tobacco, 1,600 hogsheads of beer, 50 of brandy, and the Prince's personal coach and horses.

Anchors were weighed and the huge armada was soon under way. But halfway out into the North Sea a violent north-westerly gale blew up suddenly and raged for twenty-four hours, endangering the whole expedition.

William ordered the fleet back to port. Storm damage had to be feverishly repaired, and six hundred horses, dead from suffocation when the hatches were battened down, and thrown overboard, had to be replaced. But not a man was lost, and only one ship.

When James heard that William's fleet had been driven back to port, true to form he cancelled once again the writs for the new Parliament he had called—when danger threatened—for 27th November. "The wind has declared itself popish," he laughed.

A lesser man than William might have feared to start again. But, after ten days' delay, on 1st November about 1.00 p.m., he again boarded the *Brill*, and signalled the fleet to make sail on a north-westerly course. Immingham on the south shore of the Humber estuary was the original intended landfall, and the North of England was poised to rise and receive him. But the wind veering into the north-east, carried them towards the Strait of Dover, just clear of James's men-o'-war lying well below the horizon at the Nore.

The Dutch fleet was divided into three squadrons, every ship marked by its own token. White flags flew from the *Brill* carrying William and his escorting lifeguards commanded by Count Solms; red flags denoted

William boarding his flagship the Brill *at Helvoetslys on his leaving Holland on 1st November, 1688 to invade England. His declared purpose was to preserve the liberties of the subject and the Protestant religion.*

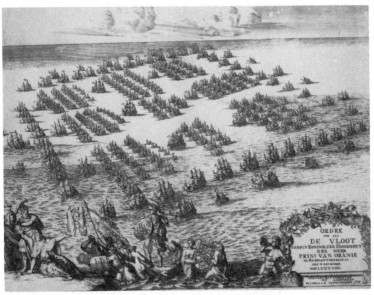

The order of William's fleet at Helvoetslys on setting sail for England. The 75 warships formed a rampart around nearly 400 supply ships and troop transports.

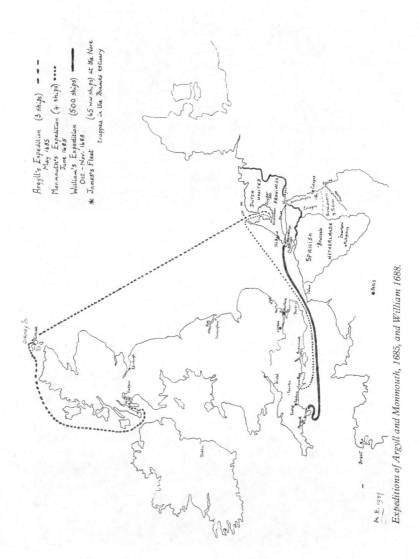

Expeditions of Argyll and Monmouth, 1685, and William 1688.

the English and Scots regiments commanded by Maj. General Hugh Mackay; and blue flags signified the Dutch troops commanded by Colonel Nassau.

The supply and service ships were massed in the centre of the fleet, encircled by a floating rampart of the seventy-five warships and frigates. At the darkening all lit their lanterns—three for the Prince's ships, two each for the seventy-five warships, and one each for the transports and supply ships. The black November night sea danced with twinkling lights like the firmament afloat.

With his keen understanding of men, William had appointed Admiral Herbert as overall commander of the fleet, for two good reasons. The British troops in the transports might have resented taking orders from a Dutchman; and, if battle was joined with the English ships and victory went to the Dutch, the royal navy would not so much resent being defeated by a commander who was one of their own.

Further, if his attempted *coup* came off, William would need to command the respect and allegiance of these same royal navy officers and men, who would then become his subjects, and they would have suffered defeat, not at his hand but from their own Admiral.

In overall command of the army under William however, was the veteran Marshal, Count Schomburg (1615-1690), a French Protestant Huguenot of German birth and already aged seventy-three, universally renowned and respected throughout Europe for his military and diplomatic prowess—so much so indeed that Louis XIV had made him a Marshal of France. But, in the persecutions following the revocation of the Edict of Nantes, he fled to Berlin, and William had invited him to Holland in July 1688 to request him to undertake the projected invasion of England.

The voyage was not top secret, all Europe was agog for it, watching for the east wind. On 3rd November the great array reached the Strait of Dover. The shoreline on both sides was black with people gathered to see the spectacular sight of "the Protestant Armada" under sail westwards to invade England by invitation!

An army chaplain on board has left us a vivid eye-witness description of the spectacle. "The whole Channel was bespangled with beautiful ships and colours flying."*

That night, 3rd November, James was told that the Dutch fleet had

*Whittle's Exact Diary (Bodleian).

passed the Strait of Dover. He ordered Lord Dartmouth to give chase; but the same east wind which had carried William's ships spanking past Dover kept the royal navy's sails bottled up in the Thames estuary.

CHAPTER FIFTEEN

William Lands at Brixham

On 4th November, as the Isle of Wight was sighted, some thought William would try to land at Portsmouth. It was his 38th birthday and his wedding anniversary. But James had a strong garrison there commanded by his natural son the eighteen-year-old Duke of Berwick. Besides, it was a Sunday and the Prince properly observed the Lord's Day quietly, attending Divine service on board with his officers.

The fleet was carried down the Channel by a wind so favourable to William's cause that it was called "the Protestant wind". For, blowing strongly from the east, it drove the Prince's ships as smartly westward as it kept James's sails penned up in the Thames estuary. Then, when the Dutch canvas had been carried too far in the night, and too near a well-garrisoned Plymouth under the command of the Earl of Bath, it veered round into the south-west and steered the whole expedition neatly back into Torbay as by some unseen hand, simultaneously checking the pursuit of the English ships down the Channel.

Monday, 5th November dawned foggy and still. Sea and shore were obscured. But the sun and a light breeze soon dispersed the mists, revealing to the astonished country folk of those parts the spectacle of the beflagged Dutch masts and sails crowded into Torbay, flank to flank, many including the *Brill* a mere stone's throw from the shore.

The forest of white flags fluttering from the supply ships raised the frightened cry on the cliff-tops that the French had come—invasion and occupation by the French to impose popery in England had been a constant nightmare to the ordinary people for nearly twenty years.

But a chaplain, mounting the top deck of the *Golden Sun* as it nudged the shore, waved a Bible and hollered that it was the Prince of Orange come to save the Protestant religion. Whereupon the cliff-top crowds burst into cheers, waving their hats in the air.

William ordered a large white flag to be hoisted at his mast head to signify that he came in peace, with a red flag below it, however, sternly to proclaim war to all who dared to oppose his mission. His standard—the arms of Nassau quartered with those of England for his Stuart wife—conveyed his message, "For the Protestant Religion and Liberty."

The very date was auspicious, the anniversary of the Gunpowder Plot, and the church bells were pealing for that deliverance from popery even as another Deliverer from the same Scarlet Woman stepped ashore.

Brixham was then no more than a little fishing village of thatched hovels, a church and an ale-house, the "Crowned Rose". It was low tide and William's landing boat, the *Princess Mary*, named for his wife and loaded with his guardsmen, could not get alongside the jetty, so it was edged in broadside on to the beach. He explained the purpose of his arrival to the quizzical villagers and was beckoned to land.

A local fisherman, Peter Varnell, waded out and, in a Raleighesque gesture, ceremonially carried him shoulder-high dryshod to the beach. William was a small man, little more than five feet tall.

The stone on which the Prince set foot in England, near the old

William of Orange landing at Brixham on 5th November, 1688, "Gunpowder Day". He was welcomed by the local Devon peasantry as a Deliverer come to save the Protestant religion and the liberties of the people. The chaplain on the right is holding up a Bible.

fishmarket, is now incorporated in a nineteenth century obelisk on the inner breakwater. The Prince's lifeguards followed him ashore, leading their horses off the boat fully saddled up and ready to mount.

It is a curious fact that the only two foreign invasions which have succeeded in landing in England—apart from parties of Norsemen and Julius Caesar—were both led by a William in pursuit of a disputed succession to the Crown, both late in the season, both having been delayed by contrary winds, both effecting a fundamental change in the Constitution, six hundred years apart—William of Normandy in 1066 and William of Orange in 1688.

CHAPTER SIXTEEN

Ship to Shore

The landing of the army started at midday on 5th November and continued all that night. Sixty boats ferried the troops from ship to shore, many men jumping in and wading to the welcome terra firma. Cheered on by drum and oboe, they scrambled up the steep rocky hillside by a track still called the *Overgang,* to what is now Furzeham Common, then arable farmland divided by "Hedges and little Stone walls." These small fields proved useful for confining the horses without having to tether them.

Here the men were mustered into their respective regiments, each commander setting up his standard in his own field. The men were "marching into Camp at all hours of the Night . . . it was no easy matter to find (their comrades) in the dark among so many thousands that continually some or other were lost and inquiring after their Regiments."

The total number of men landed was 15,400, of whom 1,100 were officers and 4,000 horsemen. Some of the latter were no doubt drivers for the draught animals which hauled the baggage wagons.

The soldiers were multi-national, a mixed bag of English, Scots, Dutch with their 200 turbanned Negro servants, Brandenburgers (Germans), Frenchmen (Huguenots), Swiss mercenaries, Swedes and even Laplanders, the latter in their striking black armour and black bearskin cloaks evoking gasps of admiration from the Devon peasantry.

Immediately grasping the local layout of the area, William ordered the supply ships to double back across Torbay to discharge the artillery, ammunition and all cumbersome equipment and stores at Topsham, the port for Exeter conveniently situated on the east side of the Exe estuary, thus cutting out a long difficult haul on the twisting muddy cart tracks of South Devon. A portable bridge, prudently shipped with the other supplies from Holland, was thrown across the Exe for the passage of the main army, when it got there, to join the baggage train.

The landing of the 4,000 horses at Brixham was not easy on such a rocky coast, and it took two days. Some local fishermen told the Prince of a nearby shelving cove where the ships could anchor in deep water yet only sixty feet from the shore. The horses were then slung out from the ships' sides in the canvas slings which had secured them in their stalls on the voyage, dropped in the water and left to swim ashore steered by men in boats with a guideline.

Not surprisingly, the poor creatures were "much out of order and sorely bruised, not able to find their legs for some days." Had the landing been contested, they would surely have been in no shape for action.

The soldiers likewise suffered "a Dissiness in their Heads, the very ground seemed to rowl up and down for some days according to the manner of the Waves", and it was "the Lord's goodness that the Foe did not come upon them at that juncture."*

That night of 5th-6th November was dry and frosty, lit only by starlight, but the ground was sodden from a recent wet spell. The soldiers, many soaked with sea water, had to stand to arms all night in case of an attack, but their presence was not contested.

They made fires from the gates and fences and "broiled" the "good Holland beef" in their "Snapsacks". Local people brought them cartloads of apples, but other provisions soon ran out and could not be had for money.

The little ale-house—the village pub—was crammed to the door with officers "so that a Man could not thrust his head in to get Bread and Ale for Mony." The landlord never had it so good—with so many lords in his house he strutted like a lord himself.

The Prince made his headquarters and hoisted his standard in the cottage of the fisherman who had carried him ashore. He slept there for two nights on his own bedding brought from the *Brill*.

*Whittle's Diary (Bodleian).

On Wednesday, 7th November he ordered the army to start for Exeter, and they footslogged ankle deep in mud well into the night. It was cold, dark and wet. The soldiers lit fires and bivouacked in their chammy leather coats on the banks of the roadside ditches, with their feet in the water; some fell asleep cushioned in the red Devon clay.

One however struck gold. He stumbled in the dark into a field of turnips, from which he and his comrades "made a brave Banquet".

One has both sympathy and admiration for the Devon farmers of those days, whose fences and gates were torn down to make fires and whose crops were raided by an invading host of 15,000 hungry young men.

CHAPTER SEVENTEEN

The Prince at Exeter

They reached Newton Abbot where the Prince's Declaration was read for the first time publicly in the market place. He lodged at Ford House, home of Sir William Courtenay. His host however, while providing ample hospitality for his guest, but fearful of James's vengeance if William's *coup* failed, prudently hedged his bet by contriving to be away from home.

On Friday, 9th November William made a ceremonial entrance into Exeter along streets lined with huge crowds cheering as if they were watching the Lord Mayor's Show. This was indeed the welcome he had been promised by ninety-five per cent of the ordinary people.

The Bishop of Exeter, Lamplugh, and the Dean had both fled in terror at William's approach, leaving the Deanery free for him to occupy. The next day Bishop Burnet read the Prince's Declaration in Exeter cathedral and on the Sunday, 11th November, he preached from the Dean's pulpit at morning service while the choirboys sang a celebratory Te Deum.

William spent twelve days in the city, establishing a bridgehead and scouring the country around for horses to replace the six hundred lost in the storm. He also ordered 6,000 pairs of boots to augment the 10,000 pairs brought from Holland.

But he was deeply mortified to find that, contrary to the assurances he had received before leaving Holland, no gentlemen of standing had joined him. He threatened that, if the Devon gentry remained aloof, he would leave them to their fate and return home whence he came. Their tardiness in declaring for him was probably because his landing had been expected in the Humber, where the leading conspirators—Danby, Devonshire, Delamere and others—were poised to raise the North.

In view of the welter of executions which had bloodied the West country only three and a half years before, after the fiasco of Monmouth's abortive bid for the Throne, the local gentry could hardly be blamed for their reluctance openly to declare their hand again for another would-be usurper likewise landing unexpectedly from Holland.

However, Sir Edward Seymour, governor of Exeter and, until James had sacked him to make way for a papist, Recorder of Totnes, saved the day by organising a formal "association" or declaration of support for William, drafted by Burnet and properly engrossed on parchment, which all who "came in" to the Prince should sign, thus pinning them down in writing to support him.

No one wanted to be the first to sign but, after the ball was rolling, equally no one wanted to be the last. The die was cast, William gave a party at the Deanery for the sixty stalwarts of Devon who had thus primed the pump and put their heads on the line by signing the "association". Among them was the Earl of Bath, commander of the royal garrison at Plymouth.

Meanwhile horsemen were off at the gallop, spurring in relays north and east. The news spread like wildfire on flying hooves that the Prince of Orange had landed in Devon and was marching on London!

The plot master-minded at the Hague in August and September now sprang into life at strategic points all over England. Delamere declared for William in Cheshire and Manchester and read the Prince's Declaration in the market place at Chester.

Devonshire likewise secured Derby, then secretly met the Yorkshireman Danby and Mr. John d'Arcy, a local gentleman, on the rain-swept Whittington Moor near Chesterfield to concert their further plans for the North. They sheltered in the back parlour of the village ale-house, the "Cock and Magpie"—ever since called Revolution House—at Whittington and plotted that Danby should first surprise the garrison at York, before Devonshire appeared at Nottingham which, being unfortified, was reckoned to be easier game.

Danby duly materialised with a hundred soldiers at the gates of York and, without so much as an argument, received the city's surrender

Revolution House, the village ale-house then called the "Cock and Pynot", local name for a magpie, at Whittington near Chesterfield. The Earls of Devonshire and Danby met here with Mr. John d'Arcy in November 1688 to concert their plans for securing York and Nottingham for the Prince of Orange. Sketch by the author after the original in Nottinghamshire County Record Office.

from its pro-James governor, Sir John Reresby, in an unexpectedly civilised and gentlemanly exchange—they were good friends—both agreeing to differ over the reason for the hand-over but not to dispute it at sword-point.

Devonshire now secured Nottingham without a clash and Delamere galloped down from Chester to join him there. On 24th November they jointly proclaimed "A Declaration of the Nobility, Gentry and Commonalty at the Rendezvous at Nottingham",* which echoed William's own Declaration and anticipated Parliament's Declaration of Right the following February.

The Lord Lieutenant of Yorkshire then brought the Three Ridings over; Lord Lumley raised the north-east and Newcastle for the Prince and the Geordies tipped a statue of James into the Tyne. The Duke of Norfolk rode with three hundred armed and mounted gentlemen into the market place at Norwich and, backed by the Mayor and Aldermen, secured East Anglia for William.

*The Declaration of Rights 1689 by Lois B. Schwoerer.

The easternmost key port of Hull was strongly garrisoned under the papist commander Lord Langdale. If William landed in Humberside he, Langdale, had ordered the sluices to be opened "to lay the country under water for some miles round that garrison."* But his Protestant officers led by Major Copley, and the magistrates of the town, conspired together to arrest him and his staff; and, on 3rd December, thereafter called "Towntaking Day", soldiers and citizens united in a loud huzza for William, the Protestant religion and a free Parliament.

Simultaneously Bristol, then the second city in England, led by its Bishop Trelawney—one of the Seven clapped into the Tower by James the previous June—opened its gates to the Earl of Shrewsbury, sent there by the Prince as governor with a company of English troops.

Lord Herbert of Charbury and Sir Edward Harley, leading the gentlemen of Somerset and Worcestershire "with a great body of Horse," took the city of Worcester for William on 25th November. Lord Herbert, "with a Party of Horse", then seized Ludlow Castle and secured Sir Walter Blunt, High Sheriff of Worcester, in that fortress.**

Over in Thames Valley, Lovelace had immediately declared for William, thus securing this vital waterway with its bridges and the castle at Oxford for the Prince. On 10th November, with seventy of the gentry of Berkshire and Oxfordshire recruited by him at his secret midsummer parties at Hurley, Lovelace galloped furiously westward to strike his sword for William. But the Duke of Beaufort, Master of the Horse and a King's man, seized him in a skirmish and clapped him up in Gloucester Castle.

Lovelace was later released under a threat from William to burn down Badminton House unless the governor let this hot potato go. Gathering his followers together, a motley crew, some riding without bridles, he galloped post haste to Oxford, where he made a triumphal entry down the High Street, now openly bedecked with orange ribands.

Back in London, Princess Anne, waiting at home in Whitehall with her bosom friend Sara Churchill, sent a letter secretly to William pledging her support and that of her husband, Prince George of Denmark.

Fortified by these assurances of support from people of substance in

*London Newsletter, 3rd November, 1688, from Earl of Powys's MSS (Historical Manuscrips Commision p.397 British Museum).
**Luttrell Collection, British Library.

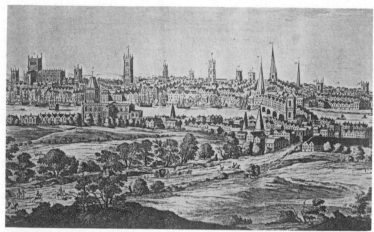

View of Bristol, 1717, then the second city in England, by J. Kip after H. Blundel. The Earl of Shrewsbury and Bishop Trelawney declared for William there in November 1688.

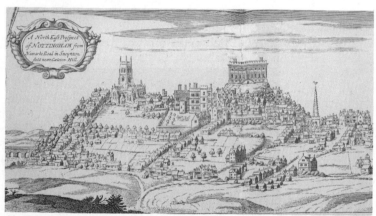

Nottingham as seen from the north-east c.1690. The stately home perched on top of the hill was then newly built by the Duke of Newcastle to replace the medieval castle.

View of Kingston-upon-Hull from the east in 1735. The moat (right, 14) protects the garrison entrance (8) and the castle (10), the blockhouse (left) guards the entrance from the Humber. The governor's house (5) is in the centre with the tower of St. Mary's Church (7) nearby. The garrison and city magistrates declared for William on 3rd December, 1688 and arrested the Catholic governor, Lord Langdale. The statue is of William III.

The City of York from the south-west in 1675. In November 1688 the governor, Sir John Reresby surrendered it to the Earl of Danby, who then declared for William. Having ridden up from Chesterfield he probably entered by the Coppergate (centre).

the realm, after the ten days of nail-biting suspense, William left his Exeter bridgehead on Wednesday, 21st November, to march to Salisbury via Axminster, Honiton and Crewkerne. Riding in the midst of his troops, his cavalcade took four days to clear the city; and the Devon roads, churned into fearful mud tracks, were solid with soldiers, artillery and baggage wagons.

Besides the 15,000 troops there were twenty-one heavy brass cannon, each hauled by sixteen horses, plus 180 smaller pieces of artillery. A weird contraption which excited gasps of wonderment from the gazers as it trundled through the villages, was a mobile smithy, fully equipped with chimney and charcoal for the repair of armament and the shoeing of horses. It must have resembled the ponderous funeral carriage of the Duke of Wellington, now to be seen at Stratfield Saye.

There was also a printing press for the propaganda war, which ran off copies of William's Declaration en route to distribute to the spectators as he passed. The Prince fully understood the value of good public relations—he had forgotten nothing.

Ladye Place, Hurley, Berkshire, Thamesside home of John, 3rd Lord Lovelace. He plotted in his cellar here under cover of a midsummer's party in 1688 to secure the Middle Thames Valley for William. The house was pulled down in 1838 and only the cellar remains.
In World War II a nearby later house, also called Ladye Place, was occupied by the U.S. Naval Intelligence and the Tudor river gate (centre), guarded by a G.I., provided as in 1688 a discreet link with London.

CHAPTER EIGHTEEN

James Goes to Salisbury

On 1st November James was shown for the first time a copy of William's Declaration, although it had been circulating surreptitiously in London since 30th September. The blood drained from his face. He threw the thing in the fire and likewise burnt as many copies as he could get hold of, keeping only one which he refused to let anyone read.

The next day he issued a proclamation, threatening dire punishment to anyone who dared to circulate or even read the document. He again promised to call a Parliament to placate the discontents, and ordered the writs to be prepared. He undertook to restore the town and city charters so recently revoked by him. He ordered the coastal lighthouses and buoys to be blacked out, and a watch to be mounted, against William's likely approach from the west, on the Thames crossings between Marlow and Chertsey.

On 17th November the King left Whitehall to join his army at Salisbury, where he arrived on the 19th after spending two nights at Windsor. He stayed at the house of the Bishop of Salisbury, Seth Ward.

But the net was closing remorselessly round him. On Wednesday, 21st November, he was invited by John Churchill, commander-in-chief of his army, to inspect his advance troops at Warminster. But, as he boarded his coach, he was seized with a violent nose-bleed, to which the poor man was subject in moments of stress, and his departure was postponed for three days. He was in truth worried sick, and with good reason. His father's fate haunted him.

A company of soldiers under Lieutenant Lord Cornbury, son and heir of the High Tory second Earl of Clarendon, had been sent to Warminster to challenge a spearhead of Orangemen, and there was a skirmish at the clash-point near Wincanton. Both parties however retired unbloodied.

On Saturday, 24th November, having recovered, the King called a council of war, and, despite strong opposition from his officers, he ordered his army to retreat to Reading. As for him, he was going straight back to London. He suspected that the visit to Warminster was really a ruse to capture him, and he may well have been right.

For that very night John Churchill left Salisbury with James's nephew the Duke of Grafton and the Earl of Berkeley, and deserted to William's camp at Crewkerne. William himself was staying near Sherborne at the home of the Earl of Bristol.

When the three defectors reported to the Prince, they found Admiral Byng already with him. The Admiral had ridden secretly from Portsmouth, unbeknown to his fleet commander Lord Dartmouth, to pledge William the support of most officers of the King's ships lying there. So now the Prince had most leading men of the King's army and of the King's navy in his pocket.

Colonel Percy Kirke, in command of the outpost at Warminster, likewise declared for William. Lord Cornbury then took the three regiments under his command there to join William's army at Honiton. However, when the other ranks discovered they had been tricked into deserting, many soldiers, more loyal than their officers, refused to change sides and returned to Salisbury. But two hundred stayed, and the defection of Clarendon's son and John Churchill helped to bring the remaining Devon gentlemen off the fence into William's camp.

On Sunday, 25th November, James left Salisbury to return to London. Dejected and confused, he stopped overnight at Andover. With him at the inn were his son-in-law Prince George of Denmark, the Duke of Ormonde and Lord Drumlanrig, son and heir of the Duke of Queensberry. The Duke was leader of the Protestant activists in Scotland. After supper, when the King had gone to bed, they too melted away into the night and rode back to Salisbury, to join William on his arrival there.

Next day James got back to Whitehall to find a final sickening shock awaiting him. Even his own daughter, the Princess Anne, had deserted him. In dressing gown and slippers, with two maidservants, she had secretly left her flat in Whitehall, "the Cockpit", that Sunday at midnight, led by Sara Churchill—who feared arrest because of her husband's defection—down a back stairs installed for that very purpose a few weeks before. The Bishop of London and the dashing young Earl of Dorset were waiting in the darkness with a hackney carriage to carry them to the Bishop's house in Aldersgate Street.

Next morning they all rode away from the City to Copt Hall, the Earl's home deep in Epping Forest, and thence on to Nottingham to join Devonshire and the other insurgents there. The Bishop himself, relishing his act, was tricked out in a buff coat and jackboots, sword and pistols swinging from his hip, passing himself off as the gallant commander of the ladies' bodyguard of gentlemen volunteers.

James was devastated. His world had collapsed around him. He was out of his depth, almost out of his mind. One son-in-law was invading his kingdom with an army of foreigners to usurp his Crown, in collusion with his elder daughter. His other son-in-law had sneaked away from him as he slept at Andover, to join his rival. Now even his younger daughter, his dearest child, had also deserted him.

His only concern now was to get his wife and their infant son, the sole legitimate male heir of the Stuart line, safely overseas, and to save his own head, the country be dammed.

Now forced into a corner, the King invited the Privy Council and representatives of the House of Lords to meet him next day, Tuesday, 27th November, in the dining room of Whitehall Palace. It was a stormy meeting; the peers felt themselves betrayed and said so. Clarendon angrily accused the King of cowardice in retreating from Salisbury when the bulk of his army there was still loyal and eager to challenge William's Dutchmen. He was urged to make three major concessions.

1. To dismiss all Roman Catholics from office.
2. To divorce himself completely from France and the French king.
3. To grant an amnesty to all who had declared for William and/or joined his army.

All were as painful for the King to hear as to contemplate, let alone grant. Next day, closetted with Halifax, he agreed to these concessions and to call a new Parliament for 13th January. But it was a mere pretence, secretly he had no intention of doing so. He told the French ambassador in so many words that he had agreed to the demands only to buy time to ship his wife and son to France, before fleeing himself to seek refuge and comfort with the French king.

He then appointed Halifax, Godolphin and Nottingham as his commissioners to treat with William.

CHAPTER NINETEEN

William Enters Salisbury

William entered Salisbury, as at Exeter, with military pageantry and to similar acclamations from the townspeople. The Bishop, outdoing the vicar of Bray, lodged him in the room newly vacated by the King. We must hope that the bed sheets were changed.

The Earl of Clarendon, having gone there from London on the pretext of visiting his estate in Wiltshire to prepare for the expected general election—cancelled by the King—now did a complete political somersault and joined his son in William's camp. The Earl of Oxford, and others of high rank, likewise jumped on the bandwagon. After the sticky start at Exeter, the fence-sitters were coming down thick and fast on to William's side.

He agreed to meet the King's commissioners, and named Hungerford as the rendezvous, conveniently situated as it is halfway between Salisbury and Oxford, where his adherents from the North were assembling, with Lovelace doing the honours there on his home ground. Here it was tentatively planned to set up a rival government to that in London, as Charles I had done in the Civil War.

The weather was good, the going over the Wiltshire chalk was firm after the Devon mud, their spirits were high and, although it entailed a diversion, the military exigencies of the day were not such as to prevent William's foreign regiments from stopping to marvel at Stonehenge, famed even then in Europe as a wonder of the world.

Late in the winter's afternoon of 6th December William entered Berkshire at Hungerford and lodged at the Bear, an old inn which Henry VIII once gave to Anne of Cleves—it still flourishes. The little town was agog with excitement. The King's commissioners had also ridden in from London!

On Saturday, 8th December they met the Prince and his principal supporters in his bedroom at the inn. But William, always aware that he was a foreigner among the Englishmen, tactfully left them to their negotiations in "the great room" of the inn and withdrew to Littlecote House, two miles away, home of the Popham family. The four-poster bed where he slept is still there.

The Bear at Hungerford, where the rival parties met in "the great room" (seen on right) at the Inn. William spent one night here. It was once given by Henry VIII to Anne of Cleves.

Littlecote House near Hungerford in Berkshire. William stayed there while his supporters parleyed with King James's commissioners in the Bear Inn.

The two sides agreed on the concessions wrung from James by the Privy Council on 27th November, with some additions, namely:

1. A new Parliament to be called.
2. Strict enforcement of the Test Act debarring Catholics from office.
3. The fleet and main fortresses in the country to be commanded by Protestants.
4. The Tower of London and Tilbury fort (both within the City limits) to be held by the City of London.
5. William to be allowed the same number of guardsmen as James, and as much revenue for his army as that granted to James.
6. While Parliament was sitting both armies to remain about thirty miles from Westminster.

This meant that William would not advance beyond Maidenhead, while James's army would have to withdraw from the capital to a Watford/Gravesend periphery.

The next day they all had Sunday lunch amicably together in the great hall at Littlecote, hung with coats of mail and yellow chammy leather from the Civil War. The party was good-natured and went with a swing. No one wanted to repeat the blood-letting of the previous generation. Under cover of the buzz, Lord Halifax, James's chief envoy, inquired privately of Bishop Burnet what terms the Prince really wanted. He was given to understand, in a whisper, that the voluntary flight of the King would be the best for all concerned, not least the country.

Meanwhile an advance party of 250 Dutch troops, probing eastwards on rumours of a plot to massacre all the Protestants in Reading, clashed with six hundred of James's Irish dragoons—the "Mounted Micks"—quartered in the town and feared and resented by the residents. The Dutch entered by the Oxford road, concealed by high hedges, and skirmished through the streets to the market place, assisted by pot shots from the townsmen watching at the windows.

William shrewdly deployed his Dutchmen against the unwanted Irish in James's army, not against the native English and Scots. Thus no one minded if the Dutch defeated the Irish.

They were routed and pursued to Twyford by the Orangemen. The dead, almost the only bloodshed of the bloodless revolution, twenty Irish and five Dutchmen, were buried together in St. Giles churchyard at Reading.

Horror stories of rumoured Irish savagery flew round Berkshire like a prairie fire. Back at Hungerford enormous fires were lit in the streets; watchmen and trained bands stood to arms all night. Weapons stored since the Civil War were brought from Littlecote, bullets and bandoliers purchased by the Town Constable; and the price of candles soared to 4s.4d. a dozen.

CHAPTER TWENTY

Flight of the Queen with the Baby Prince

Back at the ranch in Whitehall, James now arranged for the Prince of Wales to be taken to Portsmouth, where at least one friend, his natural son the Duke of Berwick, governor of the castle and commander of the garrison there, remained loyal to him. The King sent a message ahead ordering Lord Dartmouth to prepare a yacht to carry the baby to France.

But Dartmouth, King's man though he still was, was an Englishman first, and he properly refused to present the heir to the Throne as a hostage to Britain's enemy, the King of France. So the baby was rumbled back to London in the winter's night, his coach and six arriving at Whitehall in the small hours.

The next night, 9th December at midnight, in a storm of wind and rain, the Queen stole privily out of the Palace and crept down to the river steps. She was disguised as an Italian laundrymaid. With her was her midwife and the wet nurse who carried the baby Prince, the innocent cause of all her troubles. He was later known to history as the Old Pretender, father of Bonnie Prince Charlie, the Young Pretender.

Count de Lauzun, the French adventurer who had volunteered to organise her escape for the King, handed her into the tossing rowing boat which took the forlorn little party across the river to Lambeth.

Here the Queen, afraid of being recognised in the lights of the inn, huddled in the shadow of Lambeth church, clutching the baby in her arms. He was good as gold, not a whimper gave the party away the whole night. Swinging lanterns flickered fitfully in the darkness. Dim figures brought a coach and horses from the stable yard of the inn.

The fugitives clambered in and, escorted by their French pimpernel and one outrider, they rumbled off to Gravesend where a waiting sloop took them across the Channel to land at Ambleteuse, a little village near Boulogne.

After waiting a few days while carriages were procured, the refugees set off for Paris. Word of their landing had preceded them. They were met on the way by Louis XIV in person. The Sun King turned out without stint to do the Queen of England the honours in his gorgeous coach, attended by his bodyguards and courtiers in full ceremonial, riding in a train of a hundred coaches, each drawn by six horses.

On meeting Queen Mary Beatrice's bedraggled little party, at the lowest point in her fortunes, Louis XIV, the Most Christian King, descended from his coach and, with a fulsome bow, welcomed her to his kingdom with every mark of respect, and embraced the baby Prince.

He personally handed her into his own coach—the highest social honour he could bestow—for the journey to his country palace of St. Germain-en-Laye, fifteen miles north of Paris. It had been hastily and sumptuously furnished for her, complete with a nursery suite for the Prince of Wales. On arrival there she was presented with a lovely casket in which she found six hundred gold coins for spending money.

The Queen of England flees with the baby Prince of Wales from her Palace of Whitehall across the Thames to Lambeth, from where a coach carried them to Gravesend to take ship for France. The Banqueting House is seen in the background.

CHAPTER TWENTY-ONE

The King Flees

The next day, Tuesday, 10th December, James again summoned the peers to the Palace to inform them that the Queen and the Prince of Wales had fled the country. But he assured them that he would remain at his post, although secretly he was already carefully planning his own flight.

After the peers had left him, he threw the writs for the new Parliament called for 13th January into the fire. Some already sent out were then and there annulled by him in a specially prepared legal instrument. He sent orders to the Earl of Feversham, the French-born Catholic commander of the royal army since Churchill's defection, to disband the soldiers, thus irresponsibly releasing thousands of men without pay to forage for food and lodging from defenceless civilians.

He also ordered Lord Dartmouth to take the royal navy ships to Ireland, but it was too late—Dartmouth had declared for William before he received the King's letter.

James then ordered the Great Seal in its splendid pouch, richly embroidered with the Royal Arms, to be brought to him, and went to bed at ten o'clock. The gentleman of the bedchamber on duty that night was the young Duke of Northumberland, who slept on a mattress in the King's room. James told him not to open the door of the bedroom until the usual hour the next morning.

At dead of night, about 3.00 a.m., he arose, took the Great Seal, and crept on flannel foot past the sleeping Northumberland down a secret stairway to the backyard of his Palace. There Sir Edward Hales, the Catholic governor of the Tower of London, had a hackney carriage ready to take him to Millbank.

They crossed the Thames in a rowing boat to Vauxhall and the King dropped the Great Seal of England, with his own name and effigy on it, into the river midstream as they went.

It was later trawled up by some fishermen no doubt sent to look for it at low tide. The King's intention was not only to desert his kingdom but deliberately to destroy the means of governing it by his supplanter. For no law is valid until the Great Seal is affixed to the document.

A coach and horses conveyed them to Sheerness. Early on 12th

King James dropping the Great Seal into the Thames after fleeing in the night from Whitehall to Vauxhall, where a coach waited to take him to Rochester.

December, having crossed Elmley ferry to the Isle of Sheppey, they boarded "a miserable fishing boat"* which Sir Edward Hales had arranged to take the King to France. But the captain delayed sailing until ballast had been loaded and missed the tide. They had to wait till midnight for the next one.

On discovering that the King had fled, with the Great Seal, the capital was thrown into wild confusion. Consternation sat on every face. With no King, no chief executive—for the King was then his own first minister—no House of Commons, and no Great Seal the country was like a ship adrift in mid-ocean without engine, sails or rudder. Anyone who remembers the sudden abdication of Edward VIII in 1936, also on 10th December, will know the feeling.

Rumours that the disbanded Irish troops were on the rampage to massacre the population were mischievously spread, and the London mob wreaked vengeance on papists, violating their homes and firing "mass-houses" (chapels). The house of the Spanish ambassador, Ronquillo, was scandalously sacked. But not a life was taken, not a limb

*Burnet.

torn. At its most critical flash-point the English Revolution miraculously remained bloodless.

The City was plunged into "an ungovernable fermentation", and the Lord Mayor, backed by the Aldermen, called a meeting of the Privy Council, including twenty-two peers and five bishops in town, at the Guildhall that day, 11th December, with the Archbishop of Canterbury in the chair.

Having constituted themselves an emergency government, they unanimously agreed to ask the Prince of Orange, now somewhere in Berkshire, to fill the vacuum and take over the government until a Parliament could meet. They ordered all papists to be disarmed and Jesuit priests to be confined, for their own safety.

Lord Lucas seized the Tower and declared for William, the governor Sir Edward Hales* having gone away with the King. The Lord Chancellor Jeffreys, his face contorted with fear as vengeful fists pounded on the windows of his coach, sought refuge there from the fury of the mob.

CHAPTER TWENTY-TWO

William at Newbury and Abingdon

As yet unaware of these major and unexpected developments, William left Littlecote on 10th December and rode to Shaw House, a fine Carolian mansion near Newbury, then newly built by Sir Thomas Dolman, a rich clothier in the town, who first made the "dolman" sleeve.

Newbury Town Council provided horses and guides "for the Prince's use" at a cost of eleven shillings. There were no road maps or signposts in those days so guides were needed for a spearhead of Orangemen to push north to Oxford, and beyond to Brackley in Northamptonshire. At this stage things were highly fluid and a strategic link-up with the northern insurgents at Nottingham, mid-England stronghold on the Trent, was clearly envisaged.

---

*His erstwhile prisoner, Sir Bevil Skelton, was installed as governor in his place when William reached St. James's Palace.

William now received a pressing invitaton from Dean Finch, warden of All Souls College at Oxford, to dine with the university, which pledged its silver plate as financial support.

He left Shaw House immediately for Oxford and got as far as Abingdon. The town spent 14s.6d. on bellringers to peal a welcome for the Prince, and £3.17s.6d. on "sweetmeats to treat the Prince of Orange."* A roadside cottage near Chieveley on the A34 is still called Blorange House—for Bill of Orange—in his honour.

Suddenly a courier burst into the party with truly momentous news. James had fled from Whitehall the night before. The King had abdicated! He had deserted his post.

William immediately abandoned his plan to dine in Oxford and turned back for London via Wallingford.

Accompanied by Marshal Schomberg, he ate and slept at the Lamb inn there. (It is now an antique market.) They discussed the idea of refortifying Wallingford Castle, destroyed in the Civil War forty years before.

More advantageous, they now had a direct link with London in the Thames waterway, and being Dutchmen, promptly made use of it.

Wallingford Town Council hired boats for the Prince from Edward Dunn and Thos. Whitehead "to carry the Dutchmen and bread and victuals" down to Windsor, at a total cost of £19.6s.6d., thus relieving the army of much heavy transport of stores by the inadequate roads. "Wagges" for the boatowners cost 12 shillings, those for the four crewmen totalled £1.12s.0d., plus £1 for "meat and drink".* Practical co-operation such as this from the good folk of Thames Valley was one of the assets which Lord Lovelace had organised for William.

The Hurley miller, Lovelace's tenant, was one of those who opened the traps of his flash-lock to let the Dutchmen through. In all, the boats passed unhindered through about twelve flash-locks and weirs, all controlled then by the local landowners, any one of whom might have stopped them, on their way down to Windsor. Lord Lovelace had smoothed their passage.

On 12th December William left Wallingford, crossing the Thames there—as had his namesake William the Conqueror six centuries before—and stayed the next two nights at Phyllis Court at Henley, home of Sir William Whitelocke.

---

*Berkshire County Record Office.

Here on 13th December he received a deputation of Peers, Bishops and Aldermen of the City of London headed by Sir Robert Clayton, who had all ridden post-haste down from London to meet him. The first imperative was to bring James's disbanded army under control again. The Prince was therefore authorised to issue an order

> "from his Court at Henley to all Colonels and Commanders-in-chief, to call together by beat of drum, or otherwise, the officers and soldiers at convenient rendezvous, and there to keep them in good order and discipline."*

The majority, having little option, obeyed the order, but not all. Some regiments disappeared from the army lists at this time. The soldiers of the King indeed, more than many politicians, found the required shift of their allegiance from James to William a bitter pill to swallow. They resented the fact that they had been denied the chance to prove their mettle and their loyalty in a stand against the foreign invaders, a good fight frustrated by the King's order to retreat from Salisbury.**

Two days later the Prince continued along the London-bound road to Windsor—now the A423 and not much altered—making haste slowly to march with the protection of his troops. Although James had fled, William still proceeded cautiously, well aware that he was a foreigner on very thin ice.

He rode in the midst of his men preceded by a horseman bearing aloft his personal standard with its stirring slogan "The Protestant Religion and the Liberties of the Subject", and underneath his personal motto "Je maintendrai"—I secure and uphold. No plain Protestant Englishman among the staring peasants could quarrel with that.

He rode into Windsor on 14th December. The castle jostled with fence-sitters now eagerly flocking to his standard. With King James's cause apparently lost, the Prince's bid for the Throne seemed a safer bet with every hour that passed.

But suddenly a courier clattered in over the cobbles, this time with bad news. The King had been seized at Sheerness and held in an inn at Faversham by a gang of muggers demanding ransom money. Here was a pretty kettle of fish indeed!

*Clarendon's Diary.
**See page 115.

CHAPTER TWENTY-THREE

The King Mugged at Sheerness

While the smack with James aboard lay waiting for the tide at Sheerness, a gang of local fishermen, scenting booty from what they thought were fleeing Jesuit priests, had rushed the boat, got on board in the dark, manhandled the King and stolen a watch from his pocket. But his coronation ring, hidden in his underpants, escaped their magpie eyes, as did £3,000 in cash in his trunk.

They forced the terrified passengers ashore and hustled them to an inn at Faversham, demanding ransom when James was recognised. But the Earl of Winchelsea, whose home was nearby, hastening thither, removed the King to safety to the house of the mayor of Faversham.

James dispatched Lord Feversham, who had accompanied him from Vauxhall, with a letter for William to say he was returning to London to confer personally with him, but the Prince declined to see his father-in-law. Now playing from strength, he ordered that James was to be escorted back to Whitehall with all the honours due to a King.

Appropriate clothing was brought down for him to Rochester, where he had been taken to more comfortable lodgings by his companions. On Sunday afternoon, 16th December, he arrived back in Whitehall. The fickle Londoners, ever sympathetic to a loser, cheered him on his way through the City. This reception deluded him into thinking that he could yet stage a come-back, all would be forgiven.

The next day, 17th December, Dutch troops entered Chelsea and Kensington and Dutch sentinels, much to James's annoyance and painful to many Englishmen, took over the guard at Whitehall from the Coldstreams. The three English regiments in the Prince's army were posted to the Tower, the three Scottish regiments to Southwark. So the honours were fairly evenly divided.

William in fact handled the extremely delicate situation with unerring touch. On Monday, 17th December those peers already at Windsor were summoned to the castle to decide what should be done with the King. The Prince declined to take the chair, leaving it to Halifax, and withdrew from the room. At every stage in the saga he studiously left the Englishmen who had invited him over to settle their affairs themselves without his participation. He stuck throughout meticulously to the terms of his Declaration—in essence, that he had come to save the Protestant religion, not to usurp the Crown.

Plainly there could not be two Kings, one at Whitehall and one at St. James's. It was decided to send James to Ham House, home of the Earl of Lauderdale by the Thames near Richmond. But he flatly refused to go, complaining that it was cold and damp and anyway unfurnished. Fearing for his life, he requested to be sent back to Rochester instead.

On 18th December he left Whitehall for the last time, boarding the royal barge at the river steps. Escorted by ten boatloads of Dutch soldiers it slipped him down the Thames to the Medway. Defeated, dejected, and deserted by his friends and family except Berwick, he was too numbed and dazed to care.

His lodgings by the waterside at Rochester were purposely left unguarded, leaving him every opportunity to leave the country voluntarily. He did not fluff this second chance. On Saturday, 22nd December he once more rose at dead of night, and, attended only by the faithful Berwick, he stole out of the back door down to the Medway.

A small rowing boat took them to a waiting smack, its sails ready set. The unsuspecting skipper was to be shot through the head if he refused to take his King into exile. But happily the need did not arise, the revolution remained bloodless. In the bleak grey midwinter dawn the

View of Rochester in 1669. James stayed in one of these waterside houses before taking ship for France with his natural son the Duke of Berwick.

Louis XIV (right) welcomes James II to his Palace of St. Germain-en-Laye, fifteen miles from Paris, where he lived in exile until his death thirteen years later.

humble fishing boat sailed out into the Channel and thence to another sad little landing at Ambleteuse.

Although carried forth likewise furtively from his kingdom in more dignified style by a warship of the Royal Navy, one is sharply reminded of the similar unceremonious departure into exile in France, following his self-renunciation of his Throne, by Edward VIII in December 1936.

On Christmas Day 1688 King James II was joyously re-united with his Queen and baby son at St. Germains. Louis was there to welcome his cousin to his palace. The fugitive King of England bowed so low as almost to prostrate himself before the King of France.

Besides the use of the whole palace for their lifetime, Louis gave his guests £45,000 a year from the French treasury, plus £10,000 in gold coin for their immediate needs. He continued to recognise them as the rightful King and Queen Consort of Great Britain and paid them every honour due to this status, to the point of excess, even of absurdity. On his own soil Louis XIV even allowed the dethroned James II to enjoy the title of King of France and to fly the fleur-de-lys with the lions of England on his royal standard above the Palace of St. Germains.

But, after close acquaintance with him, the Frenchmen at St. Germains were privately not surprised that James was there and his son-in-law at Whitehall.

The lilies of France were then quartered with the lions of England on the Royal Arms, having been first blazoned thereon by Edward III when he laid claim to the throne of France in 1337. The title, King of France, was therefore part of the royal style and title of the Kings of Great Britain until 1801. The lilies of France were not dropped from the Royal Arms until that date.

CHAPTER TWENTY-FOUR

William at St. James's Palace

On 17th December William left Windsor to stay at Syon House, near Isleworth, as guest of the Duke of Somerset, only nine miles from Westminster and the empty Throne.

The next day, as James was borne down the Thames into exile, his son-in-law rode in a carriage into St. James's Palace; arousing some resentment however that he proceeded through the Park instead of by the open streets, where crowds in a blaze of orange ribands were waiting in pouring rain to welcome him. Even at this moment of his success, he would not play to the gallery. He had more serious things on his mind; his task was not ended, it was just beginning.

Except for the minor skirmishes at Wincanton and Reading, not a shot had been fired in the bloodless revolution.* It was a stunning feat. In six weeks he had pulled off a spectacular *coup* full in the eye of Europe, leap-frogging with a mighty fleet from the Hague to Torbay, and thence by stages with an army mostly of foreigners to London; ousted the reigning King, re-established the Protestant ascendancy and the rule of law in Britain, and restored the balance of power in Europe.

*In the nine-year Civil War 1642-51 there were fifteen battles and skirmishes in England, plus the battle of Dunbar (1650) in Scotland. After the battle of Marston Moor (1644) alone, over 4,000 corpses were buried, and the battle of Worcester (1651) produced over 2,000 Royalist dead.

It was a triumph of soldier-statesmanship by this grandson of Charles I.

On Wednesday, 19th December the Prince held court at St. James's Palace and received addresses of welcome from the Aldermen and Common Council of the City of London, from the lawyers, bishops and clergy. Only the Lord Mayor, who was ill, and the Archbishop of Canterbury, declined to attend.

He was urged by many leading lawyers to bypass the tangle of legal obstacles which confronted them and assume the Crown by right of conquest, and thereafter to legalise it by retrospective legislation, on the precedents set by Henry IV in 1399 and Henry VII in 1485 after the battle of Bosworth. But this would have flouted the terms of his own Declaration, under which he had agreed to come as a liberator not as a conqueror, to secure a free Parliament and the Protestant religion, not to usurp the Crown.

What to do then? Government was paralysed. There was no King, no Parliament, no Great Seal, no magistrates on their benches in the courts; taxes were uncollected, civil servants unpaid, and the royal army disbanded without pay. The whole machinery of government, like a tank without a crew, had ceased to function.

William himself stood exposed and impotent in a foreign no-man's-land; one wrong move by him could touch off an explosion of resentments against him from any quarter.

He hit upon an ingenious solution, fully consonant with the terms of his own Declaration, of forming an ad hoc interim parliament under whose authority a Convention Parliament—that is, one not summoned by the Sovereign—could then properly be called.

First he invited the seventy peers already in town to meet him at St. James's on 21st December to discuss what to do. He then sent them off to convene in their own House on 22nd and 24th December, and inform him of the result of their deliberations.

Next, on 23rd December, he issued a summons to all Members available from any of the Parliaments of Charles II—that of James II, which sat from May 1685 to July 1687, was held to be flawed, some Members having been unlawfully elected—to meet him at St. James's on 26th December, together with the Aldermen and fifty representatives of the Common Council of the City of London, "and hereof we desire thee not to fail"* (to attend).

The Eighteenth Century Constitution 1688-1815 by E. Neville Williams.

This ad hoc assembly of commoners thanked William for having come "for the Preservation of our Religion, Laws and Liberties, and for rescuing us from the Miseries of Popery and Slavery."* They unanimously requested him to assume forthwith the administrative and executive power in the realm.

The parliamentary Members met again on 29th December in St. Stephen's Chapel and requested him to call a Convention Parliament for 22nd January. They issued instructions on how its Members were to be elected—only by those qualified by law to vote,** and adequate notice of the election to be given, five days for the counties and boroughs, and three days for cities and universities.

Even at this late stage the Lords had tried to avoid the appearance of having renounced the reigning King by sending, on Sunday, 23rd December, a deputation led by the Catholic Sir Edward Hales to Rochester, asking, indeed begging James to come back and parley. But, consumed with fear for his life, and under pressure from his Queen to follow her overseas, he refused. That night he took ship for France.

On 29th December, while the interim Commons sat at St. Stephen's, the Lords debated with much hair-splitting how the impasse might be resolved.

Several options were mooted.

1. James to be recalled (very few voices).
2. Make William Regent for James (the favourite solution).
3. Make William King with Mary his Queen Consort.
4. Declare Mary Queen Regnant with William her Consort.

The infant Prince of Wales lying in his cradle in France, the rightful hereditary occupant of the Throne in default of his father, was simply ignored. No one spoke for him. He was indeed mentioned, but only once, and dismissed in the same breath as incapable under the Test Act to occupy the Throne, having been christened into the Church of Rome.

A vote agreeing with the interim Commons that the Throne was vacant was passed by the Lords with a majority of only three. Many peers, like many Members of the Commons, although welcoming William as chief executive, were agonised with moral scruples about renouncing their oath of allegiance to King James, being alive, and

*ibid.
**In 1689 those qualified to vote numbered only 200,000-250,000 out of a population of five million (English Parliament only).

transferring it to a supplanter. The English Revolution was really as Reluctant as it was Glorious.

For technically the Throne of Great Britain can never be vacant— "the King is dead long live the King"— and on the demise of one occupant it is automatically occupied by the next heir. But in January 1689 the King was not dead, and even if he had vacated the Throne by deserting it his legitimate son and heir, or even in default of either, the Princess Mary, was technically the occupant.

However, with the country at a standstill and the City paralysed business could not wait upon such-like legal quibbles. Now armed by the interim Commons with the necessary authority, William applied the smack of firm government. He issued orders that no Catholics were to be molested, their houses attacked or their chapels desecrated. The French ambassador was summarily ordered to leave the country within hours—protesting volubly he took coach for Dover.

The 20,000 or more Irish Catholic soldiers disbanded by James to roam the streets were rounded up and shipped off neatly out of the way to Austria, to augment the forces of the Emperor against Louis XIV.

William found only £40,000 in the Exchequer. He looked to the City, and in two days the merchants had found £200,000 for him, on no other security than his own word. That magic ingredient of stable government—confidence—was restored.

So far so good. The Parliamentarians had got their man installed in the property, now they had to establish his title to it.

CHAPTER TWENTY-FIVE

The Convention Parliament*

The Convention Parliament met on 22nd January and both Lords and Commons spent another two weeks each in their own House debating and voting upon every conceivable aspect of the Big Conundrum— whether James had abdicated or deserted, and how lawfully, or at least with a show of legality, to fill the vacant Throne.

---

*There were 513 Members of the Convention House of Commons, of whom 174 were Whigs and 156 Tories with 183 new Members.

At one stage impatience with the hair-splitting boiled over when some Whig extremists, egged on by Lord Lovelace, crowded into Old Palace Yard chanting for the Lords to declare the Prince and Princess of Orange King and Queen without more ado. Lovelace peddled a petition of 15,000 signatures to this effect.

For this outrageous pressuring of Parliament, wrestling with such weighty issues, Lovelace was summoned to St. James's Palace and severely reprimanded by the Prince; who immediately ordered the magistrates to stop all such mob demonstrations while Parliament was sitting.

In the end, after both Houses had divided and voted on every aspect of the matter, usually with narrow majorities, and the Lords had sometimes defeated the conclusions voted by the Commons, both Houses cut the Gordian knot and passed a resolution that, by his own illegal acts, James had broken the primeval contract between King and People and, having voluntarily deserted his kingdom, had abdicated the government and "the Throne is thereby vacant."

But they were not yet home and dry. Given that the Throne was vacant, how precisely and by whom was it to be filled?

When the leading peers met in the Earl of Devonshire's house to tackle this other equally hot chestnut there was still no unanimity. Indeed feelings ran higher than ever, Halifax and Danby hotly disputing the issue. Halifax would have William as Regent for James, with Mary merely his wife; Danby as vehemently pushed for Mary to be Queen Regnant in her own right, with William merely her husband. A Solomon's judgement was needed.

Solomon was duly summoned, a Dutchman in the Prince's confidence, probably Dyckveldt, his special envoy in London. He was asked to tell them exactly what William really wanted. For the inscrutable Prince, lying low in St. James's Palace and saying nothing, adamant to the last that the responsibility for settling their revolution lay with the Englishmen who had invited him to stage it, had not betrayed his inner mind by so much as the flicker of an eyelid.

The Dutchman, embarrassed as a foreigner to tell the Englishmen a home truth he knew they would not like to hear, hedged. He did not know the Prince's mind, he said, but he knew his own; and his guess was that the Prince would not have come all that way, at so much risk, merely to be his uncle's shadow or his wife's "gentleman usher".

Hearing what was afoot, William summoned Halifax, Danby and Shrewsbury and told them firmly but politely that they could if they so wished appoint a Regent, but he would not be that Regent, or merely his wife's Consort. Rather than accept a subordinate role, he would without rancour return home and leave them to settle their affairs without him.

This was in effect an ultimatum to push them to a decision, either settle the Crown on him or do without him—and that meant his wife too—altogether.

Thus the only possible solution now stood out crystal clear. William and Mary must both occupy the Throne, and both be crowned, as joint Sovereigns, equal in every respect; but, since the administrative power could not in practice be effectively divided, William would be chief executive or prime minister to run the day to day business of government.

In the words of the subsequent Declaration of Right, "the Sole and full exercise of the Regall Power be only in and executed by the said Prince of Orange in the names of the said Prince and Princess during their Joynt lives."

All three parties mainly concerned, William, the Princess Mary and equally important the Princess Anne—who now became the heiress presumptive to the Throne—signified their agreement with this arrangement, and so it was resolved.

Thus without once verbally or by physical gesture canvassing for himself to be King, William had drawn the Crown out of the uncertainties to his own head; together, with subsequent statutory limitations, most of the powers he wanted vested in it.

CHAPTER TWENTY-SIX

Joint Meeting of Lords and Commons: Bill of Rights

A joint meeting of both Houses then took place on 6th February in the Painted Chamber, then the House of Lords, to secure formal parliamentary sanction, in effect the force of law, for the resolutions passed after the searching debates of the previous two weeks.

The speeches were delivered to a packed House by Sir John Somers and Sir George Treby for the Commons and Lords Halifax and Danby for the Lords.

Three precedents, all from the Wars of the Roses, and none either happy or remotely parallel to James's voluntary flight and self-renunciation of the Crown, were cited to justify the decision to declare the Throne vacant and place William and Mary upon it. All those examples cited had usurped the Crown after violently removing their predecessors, by the simple expedient of killing them. Their title to the Crown had then been legalised by obliging Parliaments in the first Acts of their respective reigns.

Thus in 1399 Richard II was murdered by the usurper Henry IV, his Lancastrian cousin. In 1461 Henry VI was murdered at his prayers in the Tower of London by his Yorkist usurper Edward IV, and in 1485 Richard III was killed at the battle of Bosworth provoked by Lancastrian Henry VII, the Welsh Tudor usurper.

It still remained however to decide upon what conditions the Crown was jointly to be offered to the Prince and Princess of Orange.

Thus the great document known first as the *Declaration of Right,* and later enacted as the *Bill of Rights,* was thrashed out by two committees appointed by the Commons, made up of forty-three Members of the Commons—twenty-nine Whigs and fourteen Tories—plus thirteen Peers.

One committee was chaired by Sir George Treby, formerly Recorder of London and Deputy Lord Mayor, now Chief Justice and Member for Plympton (Devon); the other by the young Sir John Somers, newly elected Member for Worcester and later Lord Chancellor.

These two brilliant lawyers were the main architects of the document, together with an "inner cabinet" of six members of the two committees.* Theirs was a truly monumental task which produced a statute of monumental substance and permanence. It has stood unshaken for three hundred years as the solid rock upon which our system of parliamentary government is founded.

---

*The six were: Lord Falkland, M.P. for Great Marlow, Bucks.; Richard Hampden, M.P. for Wendover, Bucks.; Henry Pollexfen, M.P. for Exeter; Sir Richard Temple, M.P. for Buckingham borough; Hon. Thomas Wharton, M.P. for Buckingham county; Sir William Williams, M.P. for Beaumaris, Anglesey.

The Bill of Rights is in effect the working instrument of the modern British Constitution, an updated Magna Carta. It established in statute, that is, written law, the sovereignty of Parliament and freedom under the laws made by the King-in-Parliament. It made the King subject to the law, extinguishing for ever the system of royal personal rule by virtue of a mystical and questionable claim of hereditary Divine right.

It stands with Magna Carta, which in effect it re-affirms in a modern context, as the outstanding constitutional statute in our history. It is a model of brevity and clarity, its plain straightforward language devoid alike of prejudice or emotion, sentiment or partiality, compromise or dogma. It can be read and understood by the simplest mind.

The common fallacy, oft repeated even by those who should know better, that the British Constitution is unwritten, is as ignorant as it is incorrect. The main body of it may be read in the Bill of Rights, while the details—such as Habeas Corpus and the duration of a Parliament—may be found in previous or subsequent written statutes.

The present duration of a Parliament, for instance, is fixed at five years—laid down in the Parliament Act 1911—by which time a general election must be held. Habeas Corpus, which makes it unlawful to hold a person in prison without trial, was enacted in 1679.

The first half of the Bill of Rights is negative, listing James's illegal acts; the second half is positive, declaring such acts to be henceforward unlawful, such as suspending or dispensing with the laws without consent of Parliament, or arbitrarily making new laws at will by pretence of the royal prerogative, or setting up courts by royal edict other than the proper courts of law.

It also established in statute law the now familar bastions of our parliamentary system—free and frequent elections; freedom of speech and of the Press; freedom of Members to go to and from Parliament without molestation; parliamentary privilege; the right of subjects to petition the Sovereign; no standing army without consent of Parliament; no quartering of troops without consent of the householder—all now taken for granted as some of the most familiar chattels in daily use of our national scene, all "undoubted rights" and principles which were however undoubtedly only won by the Glorious Revolution, which is another reason why it was afterwards called Glorious.

The Bill of Rights outlawed the imposition of excessive bail and fines, and "cruel and unusual punishments"—that is, torture*—and reaffirmed the right to trial by jury.

It declared the right of Protestant subjects to bear arms for self-protection, "as allowed by law".

Finally, it enacted that no papist, or one who shall marry a papist, can accede to the Throne.

In the light of subsequent Catholic emancipation long since universally accepted and enjoyed, and modern thinking which allows complete freedom of conscience and worship, this may seem bigoted and archaic.

But in 1689 it was reckoned that most of the troubles of the seventeenth century between King and Parliament had been caused by the Popish sympathies of the Stuart kings, culminating in the obsessions and extremism of James II; together with the influence of their foreign Catholic wives, bringing as they did into the heart of government, then the Royal Household, their trains of papist attendants to act, or believed to act, as cover for spies and agents of foreign hostile governments, notably in those days France and Spain, not to mention the Papacy itself.

These foreign hangers-on at Court then aroused the same suspicions as do the numerous extras, far in excess of normal diplomatic requirements, which inflate the staffs of the Russian embassies in London and Washington in our own time.

A hundred years later, in 1791, most of the provisions of the British Bill of Rights were incorporated almost verbatim into the new United States Federal Constitution as the first Ten Amendments. Many of the thirteen states—the former seceding colonies who had declared their independence of the British Crown—refused to ratify the Federal Constitution and join the Union until this had been done.

Thus these two great Constitutions, the oldest in the world, which have both stood the test of time, are linked across the Atlantic by a common bond ensuring their respective liberties—namely, the Bill of Rights.

---

*Torture was already illegal in England but not yet outlawed at that time in Scotland.

CHAPTER TWENTY-SEVEN

Princess Mary Arrives at Greenwich

Princess Mary, having been delayed in Holland by ice-blocked rivers and strong westerly winds, finally arrived at Gravesend on 12th February to take her place with her husband on her father's Throne. She was met with great ceremonial by her sister Princess Anne and brother-in-law Prince George of Denmark at Greenwich.

The next day, 13th February, after a grand procession from Westminster to Whitehall with all the colour and pageantry of our State occasions, a magnificent ceremony was staged in the Banqueting House under the gorgeous painted ceilings done by Rubens fifty years before for the royal couple's grandfather Charles I, in honour of his father, James VI of Scotland and the first Stuart King of England.

William and Mary, having formally accepted the provisions of the Declaration of Right, then received the Crown offered jointly to them for life; the succession to devolve firstly upon Mary's issue, then on Princess Anne and her issue, and in default of either—and both sisters were as yet childless—on William's legitimate issue.

Princess Anne was in fact at the time pregnant with a son, born five

The Princess of Orange arrives at Greenwich, 12th February, 1689. The large white flag at the masthead of her ship proclaimed in blue letters "The Protestant Religion".

William, Duke of Gloucester, Queen Anne's son, aged ten.
He would have continued the Stuart Protestant succession
after Anne but he died in 1700, just after his eleventh
birthday. Portrait by Sir Godfrey Kneller.

months later on 24th July and named after his uncle William Henry, Duke of Gloucester. He was the only one of Anne's children from seventeen pregnancies to survive infancy, but he too died in 1700, aged eleven. His death promoted the Act of Settlement in 1701, under which, after Anne, the Crown was settled on the Protestant granddaughter of James I and VI, Sophia, wife of the Elector of Hanover, and in the event it passed to her son George I.

In a brief formal reply on behalf of Queen Mary and himself, William thanked the Lords and Gentlemen for "the greatest Proofe of the Trust you have in us that can be given", and accepted "what you have offered."

The joint sovereignty was meticulously observed. Each piece of regalia was doubled, including a second Crown regnant, and even a

The Crown of England is offered to William and Mary as joint Sovereigns in the Banqueting House in Whitehall on 13th February, 1689. The Crown of Scotland was also offered and accepted by them on 11th May, 1689.

replica Coronation chair, identical in every detail to Edward I's original—but without the Stone of Destiny underneath it—was made for Queen Mary. It has only been used once, by her. It may be seen in Westminster Abbey museum, with life-like wax effigies of the King and Queen. William, being much shorter than Mary, stands on a footstool.

CHAPTER TWENTY-EIGHT

The Convention Becomes a Legal Parliament

There still remained some loose ends to be tidied up.

The Convention Parliament, which had in effect broken the hereditary succession and bestowed the Crown as its gift upon the Prince and Princess of Orange—although claiming to act with a show of legality in accordance with the precedents cited—was not itself strictly legal, because it had not been summoned by the Sovereign, William being not yet the King when he called it.

On 23rd February therefore, a Bill enacting that the Convention was indeed a legal Parliament even though not summoned by royal writ, was passed by both Houses without a division and received the royal assent of the new joint Sovereigns, the first of their reign.

It stipulated that, after 1st March, 1689, no person should sit or vote in the Lords or Commons who had not taken the oath of allegiance to the new King and Queen. The oath was carefully worded in an attempt to make it palatable to all consciences, but was nevertheless by no means easy for many Members of the Commons and Peers to swallow.

It was in fact a double oath, the second part of which was in effect a renunciation of popery, and it departed somewhat strangely from the moderate language of the Declaration of Right to which it was appended, as if a whiff of the pent-up feelings of the time had escaped out of the bag.

However, by this stage there was little option but to swallow it. On 2nd March therefore, four hundred Members of the Commons bit the bullet and took the "Oathes", declaring that

"I A.B. do sincerely promise and sweare that I will bee faithful and beare true allegiance to their Majesties King William and Queen Mary. Soe help mee God.

"I A.B. doe sweare That I doe from my heart Abhoure, Detest, and Abjure as Impious and Hereticall this Damnable Doctrine and Position That Princes Excommunicated or Deprived by the Pope or any Authority of the see of Rome may be deposed or Murdered by their Subjects or any other whatsoever And I doe Declare That no foreign Prince Person Prelate State or Potentate hath or ought to have any Jurisdiction Power Superiority Preeminence or Authority Ecclesiasticall or Spirituall within this Realme. So help me God."

This seems to carry an echo of the Reformation and Henry VIII's Act of 1534 proclaiming England's independence from Rome; upon which, over one hundred and fifty years later, it may be said to have set the seal.

By 9th March most of the peers temporal—over a hundred—and about one third of the bishops had taken the oaths, Archbishop Sancroft however still opting out by absenting himself.

His consistency shines throughout the crisis. Having crowned and anointed James as King, and taken the oath of allegiance to him—as of course had all the Lords and Members of the Commons—the Primate could not square it with his Christian conscience to conduct the same ritual for the supplanters of that King, one of whom was the elder daughter of the displaced Sovereign.

However, both Archbishop Sancroft and Bishop Compton served together later as members of William's first Privy Council—their names head the list.

Another, non-spiritual, duty remained to be discharged. On 15th March the Commons voted without a division for the then huge sum of £600,000—three times greater than that raised for William by the City—to be paid to the States-General of the Dutch Republic to defray the expenses of William's expedition to England.

No doubt this was reckoned a fair price to pay for having removed the double threat of a one-party Catholic dictatorship in Britain and subservience to Louis XIV's overlordship of Europe.

William and Mary crowned as joint Sovereigns, 11th April, 1689. He wears St. Edward's Crown made for Charles II, she wears the Crown made for her stepmother, Mary of Modena, four years before.
The words "rightful and lawful" (Sovereigns) were omitted from the new oath of allegiance, implying that their accession was more de facto *than de* jure. *This made it easier for many to take the oath.*

The Coronation of William III and Mary II took place on 11th April, 1689, just four years after that of James II, with all the time-honoured pageantry and ceremonial, bonfires and celebrations.

Again the redoubtable Archbishop of Canterbury opted out by absenting himself, so the two Crowns* were placed upon the two royal heads by Henry Compton, Bishop of London. Although politically on the other side of the fence from the Archbishop, he too was entirely consistent throughout the crisis, according to *his* lights. It will be remembered that he was one of the Immortal Seven who had put his head on the line and signed the then highly treasonable letter of invitation to William on 30th June, 1688, only ten months before.

Thus was ended, with Parliament sovereign, the eighty years of struggle between King and Parliament for supremacy in the government of this kingdom.

CHAPTER TWENTY-NINE

The Revolution in Scotland

Scotland was no detached onlooker of the stirring events in the South. The revolution in England was exactly copied in James's northern kingdom.

Although in 1688 England and Scotland had been united under one Crown since 1603, the Scottish Parliament still sat independently in Edinburgh.** The general opposition to James's pro-Catholic pretensions was however likewise reflected in Scotland, where anti-popery at least in the Lowlands was equally vehement or more so. These were still the same breed who had shouted Catholic whore at his great-grandmother Mary Stuart, Queen of Scots.

---

*William wore the re-fashioned St. Edward's Crown made for Charles II at his Restoration and used also to crown James II. Mary wore the crown made for her step-mother Mary of Modena as Queen-consort of James II at his coronation on 23rd April, 1685. Queen Anne and George I were also crowned with the latter, since when it has not been used as a Sovereign's crown.

A second golden Orb, rather smaller than the Restoration Orb held by William, was made for Mary as Queen Regnant in her own right. All these beautiful objects may be seen among the Regalia at the Tower of London.

**The Union of the Parliaments was enacted in 1707.

James's Lord Chancellor in the Edinburgh Parliament, the Catholic Duke of Perth, was hated as much as his counterpart the Lord Chancellor Jeffreys in England. A tyrant and a torturer, he had introduced the thumbscrew to Scotland.

When news of William's progress flew north of the Border, Perth therefore thought it prudent, as Jeffreys had done under similar duress in London, to flee the city and take refuge in his own citadel of Castle Drummond in Perthshire; where however he was not welcomed even by his own retainers.

Pursued to his lair by his enemies, he fled, disguised as a woman, through deep snow to Burntisland on the Firth of Forth, where he took ship for France.

But some ruffians, following in a fast skiff and hot for booty no less than vengeance, boarded his vessel, dragged him off, and trudged him back to prison vile in Stirling Castle.

All the regular Scottish regiments, of three thousand men, had been posted south by James to contest the Dutch invasion, leaving only a small garrison in Edinburgh Castle, commanded by the Catholic Duke of Gordon, and quite inadequate for the defence of the city. So the mob, with no military to restrain them, poured forth from

View of Edinburgh from the south in 1670 by W. Hollar. The Scottish Parliament House is just below the Castle (left). Holyrood Palace is on the right, Calton Hill in the middle background.

the tenements to wreak vengeance on everything popish.

The Palace of Holyrood House, even more than St. James's in London, had become a den of popery, harbouring a Jesuit seminary and printing press. It was set upon by the mob and sacked. Huge heaps of books, beads, crucifixes and Romanist pictures were burnt in the High Street.

The Scottish Privy Council ordered all papists to be disarmed, as in London, and all Protestants to muster for the defence of their faith. The order was however pre-empted by events in the South, and the northern kingdom was already up for the Prince of Orange. A small faction of last-ditchers did indeed growl "treason" from the backwoods, but this was silenced by the general voice of support for William.

A goodly number of eminent Scotsmen had opportunely hastened on the bandwagon to London to join in the mounting general acclaim for William. He requested them to meet him on 7th January. About thirty Scottish peers and eighty gentlemen accordingly attended him at St. James's Palace, led by the Duke of Hamilton and his heir the Earl of Arran.

As he had done with their English counterparts, William asked them to consult together and advise him of their wishes, then withdrew. They requested him to call a Convention of the Scottish Estates, as he had done of the English Estates, to meet in Edinburgh on 14th March; and in the meantime, as on the English pattern, to administer the civil and military authority himself.

The Prince accepted and complied with this request; and thus henceforward all the reins of executive power in the two kingdoms of Great Britain were gathered into his hands.

The Scottish Convention Parliament was therefore a month later than the English equivalent in presenting and passing, as they duly did on 14th March, 1689, the Declaration of Right or "Claim of Right" as they called it, which recognised William and Mary as joint sovereigns.

As we have seen, the Scottish Parliament had passed an Act in 1681 guaranteeing James's succession to the Scottish Crown; but, by his illegal acts and voluntary flight from his kingdom, he was held to have forfeited that Crown also.

On 11th May, 1689 therefore, the Convention Parliament in

Edinburgh sent a deputation to London formally to offer the Crown of Scotland to William and Mary. Although neither of them ever wore it, both accepted it and jointly took a second coronation oath, also in the Banqueting House in Whitehall, that they would govern Scotland too in accordance with the Protestant religion and the laws of their northern kingdom. The nobleman who administered this second coronation oath was the 10th Earl of Argyll, son of the 9th Earl executed for his rebellion against King James four years before.

The Revolution in Scotland however was not quite so bloodless as in England. Rebellion amounting to a minor counter-revolution reared its Cavalier head in the Highlands, led by the romantically good-looking John Graham of Claverhouse, newly created Viscount Dundee by King James in 1688 and aptly called Bonnie Dundee. In the rousing words of the old Jacobite song:

> To the lairds o' Convention
> 'Twas Claverhouse spoke,
> E'er the King's Crown we break
> There are crowns to be broke,
> And each Cavalier who loves
> Honour and me
> Let him follow the bonnets
> O' Bonnie Dundee.

Towards sunset accordingly on 27th July, 1689 the 3,000-strong bonnets of Bonnie Dundee, surging south, pin-pointed with King William's forces in the rocky defile where the river Tummel tumbles steeply through the Pass of Killiecrankie, near Pitlochry in Perthshire.

A bloody clash of Highland claymores against the new-fangled English bayonets resulted in victory for the Highlanders; but also, early in the battle, the death of Bonnie Dundee. His body was carried to the nearby stronghold of Blair Castle, now the stately home of the Dukes of Athol.

The dearly-bought Jacobite triumph was however short-lived. It was reversed three weeks later after a siege and house-to-house fighting by five thousand of King William's soldiers in the neighbouring town of Dunkeld.

The "Honours of Scotland", accepted but never worn by William and Mary—the golden jewelled Crown,* Sceptre and Sword of State in

---

*Probably made for Robert the Bruce in 1306.

its crimson velvet-covered scabbard—were unused after James VI succeeded to the English Crown in 1603; except once briefly, when the Scots rejected the Cromwell Commonwealth and crowned the fugitive Charles II as King of Scotland at Scone on 1st January, 1651. But, as symbols of Scotland's nationhood, they were revered and cherished.

With Cromwell known to be coveting it, the Regalia was therefore removed for safety to Dunnottar Castle, a sea-girt fortress on the east coast of Kincardineshire just south of Stonehaven. The Castle was blockaded by Cromwell's soldiers, and the governor ordered to surrender the Regalia.

But the wife of the local minister at Kinneff, Mrs. Granger, devised a daring ruse to rescue the precious Regalia before Cromwell's men could seize it. She was admitted to the Castle on the pretext of visiting the governor's wife. Her servant carried some rolls of linen as a present for the lady's sewing requirements.

On leaving, Mrs. Granger smuggled the Crown out under her riding skirt, while the Sceptre and Sword were concealed in the remaining

The "Honours of Scotland". The Crown was probably for Robert the Bruce c.1300. The sword of state (left) is of equal antiquity. The Mace (right) was borne by the Lord High Treasurer of Scotland, Keeper of the Regalia. The magnificent gold collar was a gift to James VI of Scotland from his cousin, Queen Elizabeth I of England. In front of it is the ancient leather belt used to gird the sword of state to the King's waist.

rolls of linen carried out by the servant. The Reverend Granger then secretly buried the Regalia under a stone slab beneath the pulpit of his church at Kinneff.

After the Treaty of Union of the Scottish and English Parliaments in 1707—in which it was stipulated that the Honours must never leave Scotland—they were placed for safe keeping in an iron chest with three locks within a windowless "Crown Room" in Edinburgh Castle. The room was left unopened for 110 years, and by then the key was lost and no one knew for certain if it still contained the Regalia.

In 1817, at the instigation of Sir Walter Scott, the Prince Regent ordered the Crown Room to be opened in the presence of the Lord Provost of Edinburgh, Sir Walter Scott, and other distinguished witnesses. A blacksmith was engaged to smash the great lock of the Crown Room and the three locks of the iron chest found still intact inside.

The lid of the chest was lifted and there, under some wrappings, the golden bejewelled Regalia lay complete and unharmed, as it had been placed there in 1707. The Union Jack was run up at the Castle flagstaff to signal to the crowds anxiously watching in Princes Street that the Honours had been found, and a great cheer surged back to the Castle heights.

The Honours of Scotland are now displayed in Edinburgh Castle, together with other priceless items of the Regalia found in the iron chest—the Mace of the Lord High Treasurer of Scotland, Keeper of the Regalia, the ruby coronation ring worn by Charles II, and a magnificent golden collar given by Queen Elizabeth I to her cousin and successor, James VI of Scotland and I of England.

CHAPTER THIRTY

Counter Revolution and The Battle of the Boyne

James had unsuccessfully tried to influence the Convention Parliament by sending a letter from St. Germains, promising in effect to be a good boy if only they would recall him. But, as always his own worst enemy, he killed any chance he might have had of support for a come-back by offering a pardon to *some* of those who had conspired against him;

omitting however to name those who would not be pardoned. Since no one knew who among them would draw the fatal straw of the King's displeasure and end up on the scaffold, if James was re-instated, his letter was ignored as of no consequence.

In March 1689 however, after William and Mary had been proclaimed King and Queen in his stead, James staged a counter-revolution through Ireland. Instigated and financed to the tune of £112,000 by Louis XIV, with 10,000 men and supplies, he sailed from Brest and landed at Kinsale in County Cork. He carried the French King's own cuirass, presented to him personally by Louis as a parting gift-cum-lucky talisman on his departure from Paris—plus 14 men-o'-war, 7 frigates, 3 fire-ships, and a gold and silver dinner service.

His desperate bid to regain his Crown was not without some initial success. He was warmly welcomed on landing, and all the way up to Dublin, where he set up a Parliament under his Lord Deputy, the Earl of Tyrconnel. The southern Irish, then as now mostly Catholic, rallied eagerly to his cause. They made Limerick their citadel, disarmed all Protestants, and besieged Londonderry, where such as could of the northern Protestants had fled within the walls for protection.

The siege lasted for three months, the inhabitants reduced to eating rats in great privation, till Kirke raised it on 30th July, 1689.

In August William, now of course King William III, sent Marshal Schomburg from England with a force of 10,000 men. He landed in Belfast Lough and occupied Carrickfergus, after driving out the two regiments of James's Catholic soldiers who had held it. Then, as is all too familiar in Ireland, stalemate set it.

Eleven months later William decided that his personal intervention was needed to resolve the impasse. Leaving the management of the government in London in the capable hands of his Queen and joint Sovereign, he took a large force of 35,000 foot and cavalrymen over to Ulster to contest James's lingering threat to his kingship. William's supporters there, in effect most of the Protestants in Ireland, called themselves Orangemen, and as such the name still survives today.

Having landed at Carrickfergus on 14th June, 1690, William made his way south for Dublin, while James set off north from the city to contest his son-in-law head-on for the first and last time in a personal challenge for the Throne of Great Britain.

On 12th July, 1690, on a fine summer's morning, as his officers were preparing to join battle with James's 25-30,000 French and Irish Catholic troops, William sat down to a sumptuous picnic breakfast on the northern bank of the river Boyne. Some snipers among James's soldiers on the opposite bank, recognising him, took aim and very nearly shot him dead. The bullet however only grazed his shoulder. He survived unhurt to finish his interrupted breakfast; and later that day, in the famous battle of the Boyne, he defeated James's army and finally extinguished his uncle's hope of ever regaining his lost Crown.

But tragedy marched with triumph. Old Marshal Schomberg, caught in the thick of the fighting at the age of seventy-four, fell honourably, as the old soldier might have wished, in action.

James retreated to Dublin and from thence to Waterford, to take ship for the third time overseas, back again to France. Again William filled the vacuum—from the Boyne to Waterford he was uncontested.

Mourning the loss of his old commander, William drove on westward with his English henchman, John Churchill, and laid siege to Limerick, but failed to win it and was now himself bogged down in stalemate there.

Meanwhile Queen Mary, manfully holding the fort in London, was confronted that midsummer with a new threat from Louis XIV, taking advantage of William's absence in Ireland.

In stark contrast to Louis's inaction eighteen months before in November 1688, when not a French sail had sought to challenge the passage of William's armada down the Channel, the French fleet now crowded menacingly along the South Devon coastline over a hundred strong—77 men-o'-war and 30 fire-ships. They roundly defeated the ill-directed Anglo-Dutch fleet of 55 men-o'-war and 25 fire-ships under Admiral Herbert, now the Earl of Torrington—who was later clapped into the Tower and court-martialled for his incompetence—thus renewing the spectre of a French invasion; which, however, did not materialise.

Early in September 1690 William, tired of sitting out the impasse at Limerick, returned to London via Bristol. The Jacobite last-ditchers held out for another thirteen months, until 3rd October the following year, when they surrendered their last citadel to William's forces under the Dutchman Baron van Ginckel. He was promptly rewarded by the King and Queen with the titles Baron Aughrim and Earl of Athlone.

★   ★   ★   ★

In 1708 James Francis Edward, "the warming pan baby" now aged twenty and still called in England "the Pretended Prince of Wales", made, with the backing of Louis XIV, an abortive bid to regain his now dead father's Crown. But his attempt was doomed before it had started, when he developed measles on embarking at Dunkirk; and, although he sailed with the French invasion fleet to the Firth of Forth, no welcoming signals were echoed back from the Scottish shore, so the expedition returned ineffectually to France.

Two more Jacobite counter-revolutions, again with French backing, were staged from French soil, the first in 1715 by the Old Pretender now aged twenty-seven, and the second thirty years later by his son the Young Pretender, better known as Bonnie Prince Charlie.

Both failed miserably, not only because they were unrealistic and poorly organised, and certainly in the case of the first, half-hearted, but because Britain had become settled, prosperous and satisfied under the Protestant Hanoverian dispensation, and the system of parliamentary government and constitutional monarchy established by the Glorious Revolution and the Bill of Rights.

Louis XIV continued loyally but unrealistically to recognise the Old Pretender as King James III of England and VIII of Scotland after his father's death in 1701, until 1713 when, under the terms of the Treaty of Utrecht which ended the Marlborough wars, he was at last forced to acknowledge the Protestant succession in Britain, and forbid the Pretender to live in France.

Young James, bitterly disappointed not to be invited, because he remained a Catholic, to accede to his hereditary Throne on the death of his half-sister Queen Anne in 1714, had to seek refuge in Rome; and there, under the chancel of St. Peter's Church, he and his two sons, Bonnie Prince Charlie and Cardinal Henry Stuart, who both died without legitimate issue, are buried. Their joint tomb was restored in recent times by the generosity of Queen Elizabeth the Queen Mother, at a cost of £4,000.

The Stuart line survives tenuously, some say through the illegitimate daughter of Bonnie Prince Charlie, whom he created Duchess of Albany, and her distant posterity; but legitimately through the descendants, now living in Austria, of the younger daughter of

Henriette-Anne, Duchess of Orleans and favourite sister of Charles II and James II.

A truer blood line exists however in the family of the Dukes of Buccleuch, descended all the way in the male line from James, Duke of Monmouth and Buccleuch, eldest illegitimate son of Charles II; and back from him to the ancient Stuart kings of Scotland, to whom with their red hair they still bear a striking physical resemblance. Mary, Queen of Scots, also of course their ancestress, is the only female in the entail.

The College of William and Mary at Williamsburg, Virginia, founded in 1693 for the educational and cultural needs of the English and Dutch colonists in America, was Queen Mary's idea and promoted by her. The town, named after King William III, became the capital of Virginia in 1699, and this fine house, designed by Sir Christopher Wren, was formerly the governor's palace. Williamsburg is on the James river upstream from Jamestown, the original English settlement of 1607 and named after James I. Now restored to its 18th century character, it looks like a southern English town, with bow-fronted shops selling craft goods.

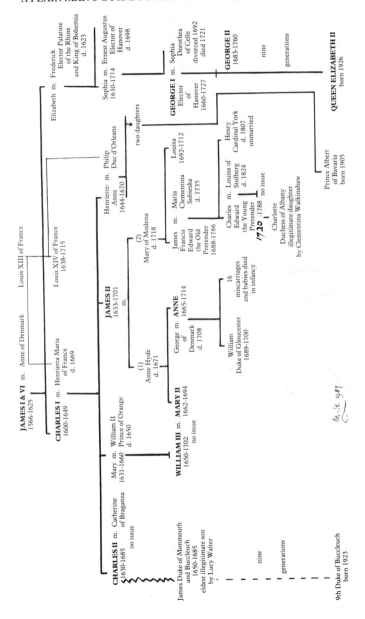

Select Bibliography

Theo Aaronson. *Kings over the Water.* Cassel 1979.

Gilbert Burnet. *History of his Own Times.* Everyman's 1979.

Sir Thomas Butler Bt. *The Crown Jewels.* Pitkin Pictorials Ltd. 1982.

Edward Dumbauld. *The Bill of Rights.* University of Oklahoma 1957.

Antonia Fraser. *King Charles II.* Weidenfield & Nicolson 1979.

Antonia Fraser. *Cromwell: Our Chief of Men.* Weidenfield & Nicolson 1973.

Allan Fea. *King Monmouth.* The Bodley Head 1902.

P. Hume Brown. *A Short History of Scotland.* New Edition by Henry W. Meikle. Oliver & Boyd 1951.

K. D. H. Haley. *William of Orange and the English Opposition 1672-74.* Oxford 1953.

Derrick R. Johnson, B.A. Cantab. *William of Orange's Expedition to England 1688.* Brixham Museum 1981.

Sir Sidney Low. *The British Constitution: Its Growth and Character.* Ernest Benn 1928.

A. B. Lyon. *The Great Seals of England.* 1887 British Museum.

Lord Macaulay. *History of England from the Accession of James II.* Longman's Green & Co. 1899 edition (2 vols.).

F. W. Maitland. *A Constitutional History of England.* 1950 edition. O.U.P.

John Miller. *James II: A Study in Kingship.* Wayland (Publishers) Ltd. 1978.

John Miller. *The Glorious Revolution.* Longman 1983.

Nesca Robb. *William of Orange: a Personal Portrait.* Heinemann 1966.

Lois B. Schwoerer. *Declaration of Rights 1689.* John Hopkins, University Press, Baltimore & London 1981.

F. C. Turner. *James II.* Eyre & Spottiswoode 1950.

Violet Wyndham. *The Protestant Duke.* Weidenfield & Nicolson 1976.

Whittle. *Exact Diary 1689.* Bodleian.

H. Neville Williams. *The Eighteenth Century Constitution 1688-1815.* Documents and Commentary C.U.P. 1960.

Henri and Barbara van der Zee. *William and Mary.* Macmillan 1973.

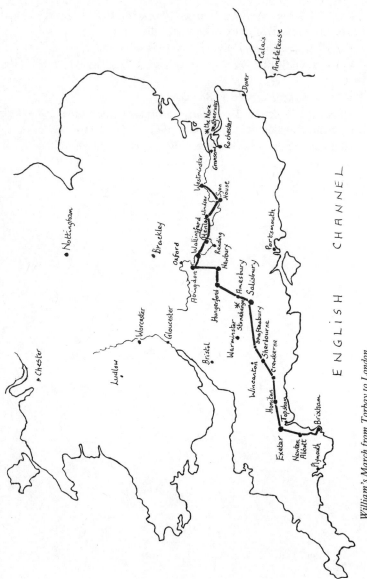

William's March from Torbay to London.

Note to para 3, page 83.

A Scottish regiment did mutiny at Ipswich in March 1689, refusing to proceed to Harwich for war service under William on the Continent. The insurrection was firmly but tactfully settled by the new King, who sent van Ginkel to deal with it, and ordered that no punishment be imposed on the rebels when they capitulated. But a Mutiny Bill was hastily introduced and enacted by Parliament before the month was out.

It was the first of subsequent formal annual measures, nowadays represented by the Defence Estimates, presented every Spring "by Command of Her Majesty" and voted by Parliament, which, in effect, sanction the required money for the armed Forces and thus ipso facto the retention of a standing or regular army by the Crown.

Before 1689 a standing army had no place in English law. It was feared by the people as a threat to liberty, a potential instrument of tyranny in the hands of the King. Hence the fears aroused by James II's suspect enlargement of the royal army, and the clause subsequently enacted in the Bill of Rights in October 1689

> "that the raising or keeping of a standing army within this kingdom in time of peace, without consent of Parliament ... is against the law."

INDEX